Prodigal, Come Home!

Facing the Facts about
Repentance and Faith

Will Simmons

First Edition: 2016

Printed in the United States of America

ISBN: 978-0-9965168-4-6

GREAT WRITING
PUBLICATIONS
www.greatwriting.org

Taylors, South Carolina

Appreciation

Will Simmons has done a good job addressing such an important issue in the realm of biblical counseling.
Here is a resource that counselors can use regularly as a tool in their ministries; I hope it receives a wide readership.

Dr. John Street, Professor and Chair of the graduate program in biblical counseling, The Master's College and Seminary, California

Dedication

This book is dedicated to the people brave enough to take an honest look at themselves in the reality that God does exist. I wrote this for you. My hope is that the light in your conscience will come on and you will take ownership of your own relationship with Jesus, through God's Word.

Chapter Contents

A Warning from God

God, after He spoke long ago to the fathers in the prophets in many portions and in many ways, in these last days has spoken to us in His Son, whom He appointed heir of all things, through whom also He made the world. And He is the radiance of His glory and the exact representation of His nature, and upholds all things by the word of His power. When He had made purification of sins, He sat down at the right hand of the Majesty on high.

For this reason we must pay much closer attention to what we have heard, so that we do not drift away from it. For if the word spoken through angels proved unalterable, and every transgression and disobedience received a just penalty, how will we escape if we neglect so great a salvation? After it was at the first spoken through the Lord, it was confirmed to us by those who heard, God also testifying with them, both by signs and wonders and by various miracles and by gifts of the Holy Spirit according to His own will.

For if we go on sinning willfully after receiving the knowledge of the truth, there no longer remains a sacrifice for sins, but a terrifying expectation of judgment and the fury of a fire which will consume the adversaries.

(Hebrews 1:1-3; 2:1-4; 10:26-27)

1

Facing the Facts, Even When They Don't Look Good

WEEK ONE

Congratulations! You've taken the brave step of actually reading this book and you have a desire to look at your life and evaluate it according to how God views it. That's not easy because most people in your situation would rather think they are normal and that it's everyone else's fault for having problems with you. Or you may be a person who has the feeling that no one in your family understands or cares about you. This book is for you. But let me tell you first that what you're about to read may highlight some things in your life that are ugly. In fact, you might even dislike what you find. But I do understand where you're coming from. I have personal experience with people like you from within my family and I have worked for many years as a counselor in this field. So I know what you're facing.

There are basically two options that lie before you. The first one is very simple: you just do nothing! You can stay where you're at, make no changes, and show no willingness to take a hard look at your life as God sees it. You simply remain in your situation, perhaps feeling as though maybe you're a victim, and that God is against you.

The second option is this: you can choose another way by taking a hard look at your heart, your thinking and your lifestyle, and then start to change—no matter the cost. If you choose this second way, it will cost you everything. But, with effort and commitment, and by God's grace, it is possible!

You may ask, *"What do you mean it will cost me everything?"* If I asked you to change just for your benefit or for the benefit of your family, all that would take place would be some reformation in your life, all to please yourself and, to a certain degree, to please others. But that is not what God wants. And that's going to be at the crux of the question you are now faced with. If you say you are a Christian, what does that really mean?

14

Is a Christian someone who just believes in God? What you are about to read will evaluate what a true Christian is according to the Bible, God's Word. You must be willing to take a hard look at your life.

EXCUSES, EXCUSES!

I was recently on patrol with a friend of mine who is a police officer in a part of a city that is high in crime. On several occasions, we received a call to special homes set aside for people who could no longer take care of themselves because of mental disorders. As we stopped at several of these throughout the day—because of fights among the residents—it was very disheartening to see how these people lived. There was such a hopelessness about them. It was very obvious from a Christian counselor's perspective what had happened to these people. All of them have been diagnosed and given the label *mental illness*, usually considered emotional syndromes or a chemical imbalance that could only be addressed by medicating them to such a degree that they displayed zombie-like behavior.

As I talked to them, each had obviously been given a certain diagnostic label by a doctor, psychiatrist or psychologist—one that would be appropriate for certain categories of their behavior. These people felt no hope of being cured. What was common to all of them was the lack of taking full responsibility for their own lives. Thus they would never deal with the real problems in their lives, and so they would become dependent on the state. As we talked to these people, there was a cold, hopeless look on their faces, as if they had given up. It was as if there was no real cure for their sick souls except the medications they used.

I've been a Christian for over forty years, and in all those years I've run across a myriad of people whose lives were full of affliction, financial ruin and deep confusion. I've seen people who were in trouble, alone, used and battered. Those whom I've known personally were considered by their family or friends as having gone literally crazy, apparently with no hope in sight. My heart aches when I talk with these poor folks who appear to be losing it mentally, emotionally and physically, especially as, over time, I watch their lives fall apart.

When it comes to people like you, one family member or friend at a time has reached out and tried to help, but, in each case, relationships have become strained and separations usually occur. You may go from one house to the next, using up their resources. But eventually everyone grows tired of the insistent arguing or strange behavior. Finally they all give up, so here you are: alone, bitter and perhaps angry, crying out that no one cares or wants to help you, seeing family and friends as your enemies when all have tried so hard.

CONSIDER MARIA

One such person I personally know and have dealt with is a good example of someone that multitudes could identify with. I'll change her name to Maria. She grew up in a home with several sisters and brothers. Their father was very domineering and their mother was quite passive. Spankings were normal, and the teaching of any Christian values was totally absent from the home. Eventually, because of the father's sinful problems, their mother divorced him and, taking the children, moved to another state. After moving, the mother had to work full time to keep the family fed, so this left the kids alone and free to do what they wanted. Eventually Maria developed a propensity towards immorality, drugs, drinking, and living on the streets. As she grew up, in time this became her lifestyle. At first she thought it was fun, but in due course it

16

became a heavy burden. She eventually married and had several children. After several years of marriage she found that her husband had been committing adultery with numerous other women, so they divorced, leaving Maria on her own, having to support her kids. She had to work, and during this time she mistreated her children. Beatings, drugs, immorality, and gang activity were her family's lifestyle. Two of her daughters moved out at sixteen years of age just to get away from her, and her two boys found life in gangs easier to deal with than living with their mom. Their lifestyles consisted of prisons, drugs, drinking, shootings, and living a bizarre lifestyle. As for Maria, she tried to escape it all by marrying a drunk. Together they fought, drank, used drugs, and lived a life full of affliction. Eventually they, too, separated, and Maria was again left on her own. Her daughters had married and moved far away from her. Her sons were often in prison, and when they were not, criminal activity filled their lives.

As Maria reached her fifties and physical maladies filled her life, one family and friend after another took her in. Each tried hard to help her, but in each case arguments, relational strains, and a strong desire on her part to live life without anyone confronting her with her problems persisted until Maria ran out of friends and family members who even wanted to help. So there she was, out on the streets with a broken car, with no money or resources, angry, bitter and with her thinking deeply warped. To Maria, everyone else had been mean to her and just didn't understand. Yet when I spoke to her, Maria really believed she was a good Christian.

This kind of perspective is very common with people like Maria. This thread is seen in the behavior of many people whose lives have spiraled down. God has revealed to us in the Scriptures what happens to people when they live a life of

17

habitual sin and, at the same time, when they think they know God personally. This kind of thinking is extremely dangerous.

Therefore God gave them over in the lusts[1] of their hearts to impurity, so that their bodies would be dishonored among them. (Romans 1:24)

The term *"gave them over"* (some Bibles translate this as "gave them up") is a judicial term in the Greek language and it carries the idea of handing over a prisoner to receive his sentence. When people consistently live in disobedience to God's Word and its principles, there will be repercussions in their lives. *Most people fail to realize that we all live in a moral universe with a moral God and because of this reality there will be reactions to every action a human commits.* And this is highly pertinent to people like Maria; they will continue to live in their sin, thinking that because they believe in God, some kind of a mystical balance will occur. In their minds, it is as though they can hold on to their sinful lifestyles and still have a free ticket to heaven. In reality, people who believe this have the kind of religious faith that demons have. James, the half-brother of Jesus, said something about this truth.

You believe that God is one. You do well; the demons also believe, and shudder. (James 2:19)

In this passage, James is referring to a truth most familiar to his Jewish readers: It's called the Shema *Yisrael* (see Deuteronomy 6:4-5)—a reference to there being just one God. This was the most basic doctrine of the Old Testament and one in

---

[1] The word "lusts" used here refers to evil or inappropriate desires.

which everyone believed. James is saying that even fallen angels believe in the oneness of God and, because of this and His greatness, they even tremble at its implications. If you think about it, even the demons have an orthodox theology—they believe the right things about God—but orthodox doctrine by itself is no proof that a person is saved. Hell is full of very smart people. Satan and all the demons know without a doubt that God exists, and they believe what He says is true and will be fulfilled just as He said. In fact, they actually know more about the spiritual realm than we humans do. But where are they going to end up? In the lake of fire forever. This is why people like Maria will be totally shocked when they die. When they do face God, they will face the judgment of God. Jesus made this perfectly clear.

> *You will know them by their fruits. Grapes are not gathered from thorn bushes nor figs from thistles, are they? So every good tree bears good fruit, but the bad tree bears bad fruit. A good tree cannot produce bad fruit, nor can a bad tree produce good fruit. Every tree that does not bear good fruit is cut down and thrown into the fire. So then, you will know them by their fruits. (Matthew 7:16-20)*

Look carefully at each word in the passage above and then take those words and compare them to your own life. What kind of fruit do you bear? The term "fruit" is a reference to your lifestyle, your thinking, and how you treat others. Look at yourself, and how you're living and how you treat others. The Bible is clear that we are to be oriented toward others and not just oriented toward self. In fact the Bible says we are to put others first, before ourselves.

19

Do nothing from selfishness or empty conceit, but with humility of mind regard one another as more important than yourselves; do not merely look out for your own personal interests, but also for the interests of others.
(Philippians 2:3-4)[2]

This is where it may get hard for most people; perhaps you have anger, bitterness, an unforgiving spirit, greed or some other habitual sin that is causing your life much trouble. Let's face it; your life is the way it is because of your sin. The Bible teaches that if we suffer, it should be because of the good we have done to others who don't follow Christ, but in your case this may not be the situation. As we will see later, there is an affliction that is caused because of sin and being honest with yourself; so the reason you're in so much trouble is because of these sinful practices in your life. What I'm asking for here is more transparency about your heart, motives and lifestyle. But, if you're not willing to take this courageous step, I can guarantee you one thing: trouble will continue to follow, a lot of affliction is heading your way, and your life will become even more miserable than it is now. So you choose: the wide road or the narrow road.

Enter through the narrow gate; for the gate is wide and the way is broad that leads to destruction, and there are many who enter through it. For the gate is small and the way is narrow that leads to life, and there are few who find it.
(Matthew 7:13-14)

Jesus is speaking some powerful words here. The words in

---

[2] See also Romans 12:10; Galatians 5:13; Ephesians 5:21; 1 Peter 5:5

their original Greek language in this verse are useful. The word *"wide"* means what it says—*wide, large, one in which many people can travel*—a reference to *the mass of humanity*. It is also interesting to know, that throughout human history, religious belief in God has been extensive, yet most people who have ever lived are in hell. It should be noted that everybody in hell may be described as religious and has a belief in God, just like the demons do. But what sets the few apart from the mass? The answer is faith and fruit. True believers have a sincere faith in God and the Messiah and are willing to be His slaves. Real faith is one that is filled with humble obedience to whatever God says, thus producing real-life fruit in a person's life.

Now honestly, look at your life. Is it one filled with righteousness, love, goodness, forgiveness, one where you put others forward before your own self, sacrificing self in the interests of others? Are you willing to give up everything to follow Jesus? Do you lead a life of death to self and of serving others for the Kingdom? Is this not what He did? He gave up His life for us so that we could be redeemed, saved from the wrath of God due to our sins. If you're going to be honest with yourself, you must realize something—your life fruit is one of no real faith or godly life fruit. You're living just like the rest of the world, perhaps striving for money through greed, willing to lie and deceive others to fulfill your own purposes, and perhaps even carrying a lot of hate or bitterness in your heart toward family, friends or maybe even toward God.

What is the source of quarrels and conflicts among you? Is not the source your pleasures that wage war in your members? You lust and do not have; so you commit murder. You are envious and cannot obtain; so you fight and quarrel. (James 4:1-2)

21

The verse above may be describing your life. People like Maria and maybe the reader, have been leading selfish lives and are now bearing the fruit of that lifestyle. You may be alone, destitute and in much turmoil. Instead of looking at yourself honestly and coming to repentance before a very loving and caring God, most people would rather stay stubbornly in their sin, blaming others and maybe even blaming God for all their problems. Is that where you're at? Look around you; stand up and go look in the mirror—that's you in all your sin. Can you imagine how God sees you? He created you and knows your every thought and intent. At the core of it all is this: you love the world and all its ways more than you love Him. You may try to fool others but God knows it all. He knows all about you; in fact He knows you better than you know yourself. You may think that your thoughts, motives and ways are somehow hidden from God, but the reality is that He is your Creator and knows all these things. Secret sins are not as secret as you may think. You may fool others, but you can't fool God.

As for you, my son Solomon, know the God of your father, and serve Him with a whole heart and a willing mind; for the LORD searches all hearts, and understands every intent of the thoughts.
(1 Chronicles 28:9)

I, the LORD, search the heart,
I test the mind,
Even to give to each man according to his ways,
According to the results of his deeds.
(Jeremiah 17:10)

"Can a man hide himself in hiding places
So I do not see him?" declares the LORD.
"Do I not fill the heavens and the earth?" declares the
LORD. (Jeremiah 23:24)

O LORD, You have searched me and known me.
You know when I sit down and when I rise up;
You understand my thought from afar.
You scrutinize my path and my lying down,
And are intimately acquainted with all my ways.
(Psalm 139:1-3)[3]

As you can see, God knows and sees everything you do. Psalm 90 was written by Moses. After going through many hardships with the people of Israel during the desert wonderings, Moses had grown old, was tired and afflicted, but besides all this, he had a great hope in God's love and mercy. Yet he realized that in all this God knew his sins and dealt with each one accordingly.

You have placed our iniquities before You,
Our secret sins in the light of Your presence. (Psalm 90:8)

All our sins are in clear view before God. So here we come to a crossroads in this book. You can either take an honest look at yourself and start dealing with all these sinful issue by repenting and choosing to do things God's way for the rest of your life. Or you can stay in the mess you're in, living in misery, and remaining under the wrath of God. Only those who choose the narrow road will actually be blessed by God and protected by

---

[3] See also Psalm 50:16-23

Him. This doesn't mean you won't go through trouble. Trouble will be there not necessarily because of sin. But if you choose to remain in all your sin, affliction will follow you, just as surely as the Hound of Heaven[4] will chase you.

If you do choose God's way, the rest of the book will be a great challenge but one in which true peace, contentment and direction in life will be yours by the power of the Spirit and the Scriptures.

What about Maria? What did she do? Sadly, she chose to stay in her sin. During those troubled times in her life, the doctor recommended that she go and see a psychiatrist. The doctor told her that all her greed, lying, hatred and bitterness toward others were not her fault. He said that they were caused by a chemical imbalance in her body and also caused by her parents. He ran no physical tests or blood panels, but instead made his decision based upon what she told him and based on his visual observations of her behavior for several minutes. His view was that she had some kind of chemical imbalance, and therefore he prescribed medications for her. He believed this would solve her problems, when in reality it did nothing to solve them because her problem was herself and her sin. Because God exists and has spoken, that means the prescription for becoming whole again is a completely different one. The prescription is repentance from a pure heart that has been humbled by God, and a desire for obedience to His Word, thus glorifying Him.

Remember that ride along I had with my friend, the police

---

[4] *Hound of Heaven*: this is a reference to a poem titled by that name, written by Francis Thompson (1859–1907), in which he wrote of how he tried to run away from God, and the claims of Christ on his life, and how he knew no peace in his life until he came to Christ in repentance and faith. Poem in full may be read here: http://www.bartleby.com/236/239.html

officer? Ultimately, God's way is the only solution to all the people's problems I saw that day. But because of society's rejection God, the Bible, and the biblical view of sin, its only solution is to use medication, something that only masks the real problems people have by sedating them. Maria did not have low self-esteem, some kind of chemical imbalance or syndrome; she had a sin problem.

Did you ever notice the middle letter in sin is "I"? That's the problem with everyone. "I want this, I want that, I want my way and if people don't conform to that, then conflict, anger and greed take over." But why do so many people succumb to these psychological labels? Because, at first, it may appear it is a much easier way than dealing with their sin. However, when a person chooses to do things God's way, the process of change through the power of the Spirit in obedience to His Word starts, and change for the better occurs. It is from here that God starts his sanctifying work in their lives, pushing them towards Christlike ways of living.

Dear reader, do you want to stay in the mess you're in, or do you want to change to really do things God's way and have peace? God's way is always the best.

Maria chose the medications as solution to all her life problems. But all this did was cover up the reality that she needed to deal with her relationship with the Lord and deal with her sin. As time passed, things became worse. Eventually she stopped taking the medications because her problems were ongoing. She is still on the streets, living in her broken-down car, bitter, angry, and trying to find ways to make some money. She once told me, *"This is all God's fault; He is doing all this against me."* This is the plight of anyone who sets aside God's way and instead walks in habitual sins.

LET'S BE REAL

One of the common behaviors among people like Maria is their twisted view of what truth is, what and who God is, and what He actually expects of them. In counseling people, I have found that one of the most common features of their behavior is the lack of a correct biblical view of these things and, depending on how old and long they have been this way, their lack of desire to turn away from the destructive ways of this kind of lifestyle. Prodigals have a natural tendency to strip God of His majesty, power and reverence in order to bring Him down to being almost like us (Psalm 50:21). Why? Accountability! Prodigals want to get away with their irresponsibility and sin so, if they can reduce God to being like us, He becomes our buddy, our equal, and so, they reason, He would never judge them. This watered-down view of God is just one big lie and will all fall apart in the end.

In order for troubled people to understand who they really are before a Holy God, they need to see how God views us all. Why? Because in Maria's eyes, she saw herself as basically a good person and, due to her goodness, one who would go to heaven. But reality is quite different! I've never met a prodigal who has a correct view of God, sin, forgiveness, and especially of regeneration. All the prodigals I have met totally lacked a correct view of themselves as God sees them. So, in order to help the reader know this, let's take a tour through Scripture and see what God thinks about us all.

A GOD'S-EYE VIEW

Let's see what God has said about you and the whole human race. What does God think of us? Does He think we are great? Good? Do we have a chance of getting some favors from Him if we act or do well? Let's find out. The following is from God Himself concerning the reader and everybody else on the earth, now and the past. The comments I make will strictly be in reference to the context of what God has said in His Word (the Bible). I will not be giving my opinion. The reason I bring this to the reader is because the core reason for people's problems is threefold:

- **First**, they usually think somehow God will overlook their sin because of all their sufferings and because of all the good things they have done.
- **Second**, they may think God is too loving and good to send a person like Maria to hell and that somehow they deserve better.
- **Third**, the reason they are caught up in their sin is because of selfishness and pride. Most people have created a self-centered lifestyle where anger, greed and other kinds of sins have become a normal pattern of behavior and are therefore totally acceptable.

For people like Maria, the connection between a sinful lifestyle and God's wrath upon sin is missing. That's a dangerous place to be! God loves people, but He is also a righteous judge, and by both His nature and Word He will judge all sin.

But, let me warn the reader. After years of study on this subject, I have found that God's views may contradict what the reader thinks of himself or others. The world has so influenced the church that even terms such as self-esteem, self-worth, or our worthiness before God are all fully accepted as basic Christian values. In reality, these terms are totally unbiblical.

This was Maria's problem; she thought she deserved more than she had. For the reader, you may not like what God says, but remember this question: *Who is your authority?* If God is, then it doesn't matter what you think. In a much lesser example, it would be like a six-year-old boy going up to the President of the United States and telling him what to do about the arms race. That would be ridiculous! So there is a parallel for the person who thinks he can ignore God and believe his own way. If God decrees something, then it will happen, and no one can prevent His will, no matter how powerful, how intelligent or how rich that person may be. No human has the ability to take the place of God. Instead, true believers will desire to align themselves with God's will, no matter the cost. The Creator is always greater than the creation! God said this startling thing:

> *The fool has said in his heart, "There is no God."*
> *They are corrupt, they have committed abominable deeds;*
> *There is no one who does good.*
> *The LORD has looked down from heaven upon the sons of men*
> *To see if there are any who understand,*
> *Who seek after God.*
> *They have all turned aside, together they have become corrupt;*
> *There is no one who does good, not even one. (Psalm 14:1-3)*

So if you're still brave enough to read on—congratulations! Here is what God thinks of us. First I will quote God, and then discuss what He said.

WHAT ARE WE WORTH?

This is where modern society's view of people has infiltrated the church to such a great extent that matters like self-image, self-esteem, and self-worth are themes found everywhere. Pride is at the core of it all, and it is so much the opposite of a truly biblical Christian attitude. Instead of thinking we are worth something, instead of feeling the need to be at the center of the universe, we should realize that God is not impressed! Instead He sees us all as totally worthless. He is the Master who brings people like us out of the slave market of sin. By nature, we are slaves!

"What is man, that he should be pure,
Or he who is born of a woman, that he should be righteous?
"Behold, He puts no trust in His holy ones,
And the heavens are not pure in His sight;
How much less one who is detestable and corrupt,
Man, who drinks iniquity like water! (Job 15:14-16)

"How then can a man be just with God?
Or how can he be clean who is born of woman?
"If even the moon has no brightness
And the stars are not pure in His sight,
How much less man, that maggot,
And the son of man, that worm!" (Job 25:4-6)

And although you were formerly alienated and hostile in
mind, engaged in evil deeds, 22 yet He has now reconciled
you in His fleshly body through death, in order to present
you before Him holy and blameless and beyond reproach.
(Colossians 1: 21-22)

"The heart is more deceitful than all else
And is desperately sick;
Who can understand it?
"I, the LORD, search the heart,
I test the mind,
Even to give to each man according to his ways,

29

According to the results of his deeds. (Jeremiah 17: 9-10)

You are of your father the devil, and you want to do the desires of your father. (John 8:44)

...for all have sinned and fall short of the glory of God... (Romans 3:23)

These few Scriptures quickly reveal to us the pure holiness of God and our utter sinfulness. And deep down inside, as we read these Scriptures, we know it. In the depths of our being, we know something is wrong with us. Why? Because our conscience is constantly bearing witness that we are all sinful creatures. We might try to blame others or put psychological labels on our behavior or even say that we have low self-esteem, but the reality is we are sinners and we have become unclean in the sight of God. It's almost impossible to deny our own consciences unless we come to the point—a very danger-ous point—in which our consciences become dead. The idea of self-esteem might try to sweep all this away in our minds or we may seek comfort in other relationships, or blame all our problems on someone else. This might make us feel a little better for a short time, but the relief is always superficial. The reality is that we are heaping guilt upon ourselves and not being honest about our pride of sin. When we feel guilty, there is only one cause so we must realize the existence of sin, and realize that God exists and will hold everyone accountable. So it is sin—not low self-esteem—which is the very answer that the gospel outlines.

A HIDDEN BIAS

Then the LORD saw that the wickedness of man was great

on the earth, and that every intent of the thoughts of his
heart was only evil continually. (Genesis 6:5)

The wickedness of early mankind was great and God saw all people as naturally evil. They were fleshly and lived in their sins (see Genesis 6:3). They were totally sensual, the desires of their mind overwhelmed them, they were totally lost in the desires of the flesh, and their souls no longer discerned God's ways. They were ever desiring earthly things, so that they were sensualized, brutalized, and no longer retaining God in their knowledge, but living according to their own ways in this life. Throughout history, people have consistently been like this. Because of greed, sensual desires, a lust for power and authority, man has brutalized others until our own day.

The Scripture referred to above shows that people lived in a state of total wickedness. All was corrupt within, and all unrighteous without. This wickedness was great (Hebrew, "rabbah") "was multiplied;" it was continually increasing so that the whole earth was corrupt before God, and was filled with violence (Genesis 6:11). Can you imagine how terrible it must have been to live during that time? All the imaginations of their thoughts were evil continually. From young to old, every thought, conception, and ideas that were formed were all evil. The fountain which produced them was completely poisoned by sin. All these were evil without any mixture of good. The Spirit of God strove to restrain sin, but He was continually resisted, so evil had its ways. People were evil continually—there was no interval of good, no moment allowed for serious reflection, no holy desires, and no righteous act. What a terrible picture of fallen souls! And to think that during times such as these Adam and Eve, Job and Noah were probably living. This is such a picture only God—who searches the

31

heart and tries the spirit—could possibly give. This is the state of every human born, as it is even today in our societies. God sees every human existing bent naturally toward sin.

The heart is more deceitful than all else
And is desperately sick;
Who can understand it?
"I, the LORD, search the heart,
I test the mind." (Jeremiah 17:9-10)

"Though I am righteous, my mouth will condemn me;
Though I am guiltless, He will declare me guilty. (Job 9:20)

The LORD knows the thoughts of man,
That they are a mere breath. (Psalm 94:11)

Who can say, "I have cleansed my heart,
I am pure from my sin"? (Proverbs 20:9)

Indeed, there is not a righteous man on earth
who continually does good and who never sins.
(Ecclesiastes 7:20)

...for all have sinned and fall short of the glory of God...
(Romans 3:23)

If we say that we have no sin, we are deceiving ourselves
and the truth is not in us. (1 John 1:8)

The verses above explain the true picture of our lost state and the reality that every single one of us deserves hell. There is absolutely nothing within us in our natural state that is good and glorifies God. At this point, lost people remain under the wrath of God. But there is a great hope for us—not from within ourselves, but from outside, all by the work of Christ on the cross. But there will always be this large mass of people alive in every generation, people like Maria, who are living as these others in the past have lived. These in the past had the personal testimonies of Adam and Eve, Noah and Job, yet still they resisted. Today people like Maria have preachers of the gospel, sound Christian books, TV, and personal testimonies of family and friends around them—yet still they resist. They resist because they think all is well between them and God, not realizing God's wrath hangs over their heads. For the people in the past, there was a flood; for those today, a fire upon the earth is imminent. (See 2 Peter 3:10-11.)

IS MY "GOOD" GOOD ENOUGH FOR GOD?

> *For all of us have become like one who is unclean,*
> *And all our righteous deeds are like a filthy garment;*
> *And all of us wither like a leaf,*
> *And our iniquities, like the wind, take us away.*
> *(Isaiah 64:6)*

Our performances—though they may be ever so good—if we depend upon them for our righteousness and think they will be of merit us, are as filthy rags when compared to God's holiness. No one can dwell in His presence if they are trusting in them. Our best deeds are so defective, and so below God's perfect standards, that they are as filthy rags, full of sin and corruption. When we would do good, evil is present with us; and the iniquity of our lives would be our ruin if it were not for God's grace, Christ's work, and the Spirit's power at work in us.

I have a friend who lives out this philosophy. She thinks that because she is basically good and that because she has never robbed a bank or killed anyone, these so-called good qualities all count toward her free ticket to heaven. She believes that God is too loving to send a good person to hell. The reality of this is startling. The Apostle Paul was a man who had much to brag about, especially being outwardly good. He mentioned this in his letter to the Philippians.

> *For we are the true circumcision, who worship in the Spirit of God and glory in Christ Jesus and put no confidence in the flesh, although I myself might have confidence even in the flesh. If anyone else has a mind to put confidence in the flesh, I far more: circumcised the eighth day, of the nation of Israel, of the tribe of Benjamin, a Hebrew of Hebrews; as to the Law, a Pharisee; as to zeal, a persecutor of the church; as to the righteousness which is in the Law, found blameless.*
>
> *But whatever things were gain to me, those things I have counted as loss for the sake of Christ. More than that, I count all things to be loss in view of the surpassing value of knowing Christ Jesus my Lord, for whom I have suffered the loss of all things, and count them but rubbish so that I may gain Christ... (Philippians 3: 3-8)*

As you can see, if anyone had anything to brag about, it would have been the Apostle Paul, and if any man could say he was good, he would have been the man. But Paul had a biblical perspective on human goodness. The Greek word Paul uses for *"gain"* is an accounting term that means profit. The Greek word for *"loss"* is also an accounting term used to describe a business loss. Paul used the language of the business world of his day to describe the spiritual transactions that occurred when Christ redeemed him. Before Paul's conversion, he was a very proud religious man, who thought all his good works would get him to heaven. He believed that they would all be of profit to his spiritual bank account. Yet in reality, they were worthless and damning. Once he was reconciled to God, he put all his good works in his loss column when he compared himself to all the glories of Christ and God's requirements for entering heaven.

Jesus also spoke about this, saying:

And He also told this parable to some people who trusted in themselves that they were righteous, and viewed others with contempt: "Two men went up into the temple to pray, one a Pharisee and the other a tax collector. The Pharisee stood and was praying this to himself: 'God, I thank You that I am not like other people: swindlers, unjust, adulterers, or even like this tax collector. I fast twice a week; I pay tithes of all that I get.' But the tax collector, standing some distance away, was even unwilling to lift up his eyes to heaven, but was beating his breast, saying, 'God, be merciful to me, the sinner!' I tell you, this man went to his house justified rather than the other; for everyone who exalts himself will be humbled, but he who humbles himself will be exalted." (Luke 18:9-14)

This parable of Jesus recorded by Luke clearly shows that a person can be very good, even good in a religious way, and looked upon by others as their standard. Yet in reality, these people are totally lost and heading to hell. The parable was addressed to those who trusted in themselves and their good works, as if this would cause them to merit heaven. But the best human goodness, even the goodness of a Pharisee, falls far short of the divine standard.

So you might ask the question, "What is God's standard?" Jesus gives us that standard in Matthew 5:48, *"Therefore you are to be perfect, as your heavenly Father is perfect."* That is the standard you must meet if you are to get to heaven. In reality, you'll never make it; no one will. The reason you're reading this book is because you have missed that mark already, just like everyone else has. So, in one way, you have no hope if you're trying to earn your way to heaven, as you will fail and end up eternally separated from God and in hell. God won't lower His standard without compromising His own holiness and perfection. He who is perfect could not set an imperfect standard for entering heaven. But that's what the marvelous truth of the gospel is all about. It's good news, that Christ has met this standard on behalf of people like you. *"He made Him who knew no sin to be sin on our behalf, so that we might become the righteousness of God in Him."* (2 Corinthians 5:21).

Here in this verse, Paul summarizes the very heart of the gospel to you, the good news, explaining how sinners like you and I can be reconciled to God through Jesus Christ. Jesus was sinless; therefore He became the perfect sacrifice for your sentence. It was on your behalf. God took His righteousness and it can be imputed to you. The wrath that sinners deserve was exhausted upon Jesus at the cross, and thus He met all the requirements of God's law when He died. When the Bible discusses the righteousness of God, it's just another reference to justification and imputation. In other words, God may credit to your account what Jesus did, and so you may become righteous before God. He bore our sins so that we could bear his righteousness. God treated Him as if He committed the believer's sins, and He treats believers as if they had only done the righteous deeds of the sinless Son of God. So you see it had nothing to do with you and all your good deeds; it has everything to do with putting your trust in Christ and His work on the cross on your behalf, and putting faith in Him. Your part is to have faith, and the fruit of this should be a pursuit of holiness in your life out of a heart of love for what God has done for people like you, people who deserved eternal hell. But to do this you must be willing to understand your miserable plight and be willing to give up all to follow Christ.

THE WALKING DEAD?

There is a sense in which God sees people as walking dead men, alive on this earth but dead to Him. This is so of every human. This particular subject must be explained. Anthropology—the science and study of man—is usually approached from two different angles. First is the humanistic approach, usually through man-centered philosophy; the second approach is from the Scriptures. The first avoids anything to do with God or the Bible, whereas, through the Scriptures which are *"God-breathed,"* the second looks at and defines man's past existence, present condition, and future existence. The first is created by man, a reflection of his own philosophy of life; the other is the very revelation of God Himself to people.

It is the second approach that is the more practical to prodigals. The influence of man and his humanistic philosophy finding its way into the church is profoundly important. A correct view of ourselves is essential if we are to have a correct view of humanity as a whole. If one's view in this area lacks biblical clarity, definitions of (and solutions to) problems will be skewed and wrong.

But the issues are deeper than what has been mentioned above. For at the heart of the question is that part of man that has the ability to live forever—his human spirit. In the humanist's view, man's immaterial part is recast to fit the present lifestyle he leads—that is, one of sin. But for the believer, sin is something that penetrates much deeper than the patterns of a lifestyle. Sin is something that completely affects the human heart.

Man is defined biblically as a fallen creature, degraded by sin, yet intended by God to be saved, redeemed and eternally secure. But most people find this view of change hard to accept. Man has a dual nature, unlike everything else God created. There is the material and the immaterial part of man, the physical body and the human spirit. The creation of Adam involved an *"inbreathing of life"* (see Genesis 2:7) making him a living soul, different from all the other physical, animal and plant creation around him. Mankind was made in the image of God. Concerning this important area of *"in-breathing,"* there are several Scriptures that give us a correct view of man.

- Man became a living soul. His "humanness" took on life. The very opposite of death, he breathes, moves and thinks (Genesis 1, 1 Corinthians 15:47-49, Genesis 3:19). Adam was made of dust—that is, the material side of man. When God created Adam, he was a body made of flesh and bone. It wasn't until He instilled the human spirit—the soul—that Adam became a living human. And unlike the rest of created things and animals, Adam could relate to his Maker.
- This inbreathing from God is what defines the real person. It is the part that will exist forever—either in hell or heaven. Man has a human spirit, that part of him that sets him apart from the rest of creation. It is that part of him that is most important to God and to man's future state. The human spirit is regenerated by the Spirit when a person comes to Christ and He comes to actually dwell within. (See

James 2:26, 2 Corinthians 5:6-8, Matthew 10:28, Hebrews 9:27.)

- What of the future state of the human spirit, that immaterial side of man? This is the final chapter in the view of man. It is man, the human spirit, that stands before God, either redeemed through Christ or condemned for sin to eternal separation from God. God's holy and righteous judgment means being eternally separated from all the blessings there might otherwise have been. But for the redeemed, there will be eternal bliss on a new earth, and with no more sickness and suffering. There will be new immortal bodies that have the ability to live forever on the new earth (Revelation 21). The new earth will be a restored Eden without the snake, the final place of the redeemed humans. (See John 5:26-29, Daniel 12:2, Revelation 20:12, 1 Corinthians 15:51-53.)

This short and concise study of man looks at the true nature of man's existence, his present condition of sin and his future. If a person has a biblical view of who he is, he will shun the worldly views that have so easily crept into our churches and he will throw off such humanistic views such as self-worth, self-image, self-esteem, blaming his problems on others, and all the evolutionary explanations thrown at believers. Instead, he will become a responsible person, realizing the truths of Scripture concerning himself. This is exactly the opposite of what troubled people do. That's why there are so many problems in their lives.

In this, and this alone, is a true view of mankind found. And within this biblical view can anyone look at himself honestly and see what needs to be done? If you are like Maria, and realize the great accountability we all have before God our Creator, you must come to Him. It is here you'll find true hope for your life.

39

FOLLY

God sees the human race as people who consistently seek out foolish ideas about Him, about themselves, and where truth is found. People tend to naturally create their own kind of "holy truth" or try to find it by some mystical, inward journey, instead of an outward search for God and what He has already revealed in the Scriptures. The problem with people in trouble isn't the need for new revelation from God through some mystical or experiential moment; instead what they need is a return to the one constant, the source of all truth—the Bible. In this you will find both true salvation in Christ and clear direction in life. But the question has to be asked: why are people so foolish when it comes to God and what He wants? There are three basic reasons why people look everywhere but in the right place:

- People desire to leave God out of their lives because it will cost too much to follow Him. A complete surrender to Christ as Master is far beyond what they are ever willing to go; this lies at the core of it all.
- People desire to seek other foolish answers instead of God's ultimate solutions for life because the ones they make up are easier, allowing them to remain in their sinful state with little accountability and perhaps still seemingly in a relationship with God.
- People think that just "believing" God exists is good enough. This is an extremely common view. But as discussed earlier, this head-knowledge that God exists will result in nothing more than the same knowledge that demons have—and that is not too encouraging!

Honestly, is this where you are? Read the verses below and

use them to gauge where you are at this stage in your life.

The fool has said in his heart, "There is no God."
They are corrupt, they have committed abominable deeds;
There is no one who does good.
The LORD has looked down from heaven upon the sons of men
To see if there are any who understand,
Who seek after God.
They have all turned aside, together they have become corrupt;
There is no one who does good, not even one. (Psalm 14:1-3)

God has looked down from heaven upon the sons of men
To see if there is anyone who understands,
Who seeks after God.
Every one of them has turned aside; together they have become corrupt;
There is no one who does good, not even one. (Psalm 53:2-3)

"How long, O naive ones, will you love being simple-minded?
And scoffers delight themselves in scoffing
And fools hate knowledge?
Turn to my reproof..." (Proverbs 1:22-23)

"Everyone who hears these words of Mine and does not act on them, will be like a foolish man who built his house on the sand. The rain fell, and the floods came, and the winds blew and slammed against that house; and it fell—and great was its fall." (Matthew 7:26-27)

For we also once were foolish ourselves, disobedient, deceived, enslaved to various lusts and pleasures, spending our life in malice and envy, hateful, hating one another. But when the kindness of God our Savior and His love for mankind appeared, He saved us, not on the basis of deeds which we have done in righteousness, but according to His mercy, by the washing of regeneration and renewing by the Holy Spirit, whom He poured out upon us richly through Jesus Christ our Savior, so that being justified by His grace we would be made heirs according to the hope of eternal life. (Titus 3:3-7)

As you have just read these verses and compared them to your life, is it a coincidence that you are having so much trouble? Foolish people do foolish things, say foolish words, and think foolishly, leading to a foolish lifestyle. Take a hard look at your lifestyle: is it foolish? Be honest: are the things that you say, think, and live glorifying God in heaven? I would venture to say no! This is why you're in so much trouble. It's a dangerous place to be thinking you're a Christian when in reality you're lost and separated from God. Yes, you might believe in God and even be religious once in a while, but that doesn't mean you're saved from God's wrath on sin. If you deny everything I've said so far, then there is little hope for you and your life. But, if you're serious about your relationship with Christ and you want to have a clear conscience, peace with God, and real direction in life, it must start with you realizing the ugly truth about yourself. You are a sinner and you have trained yourself to walk in habitual sin. If you were to die tonight, you would wake up to know you would be in hell forever and ever.

But there is hope; in fact, there is tremendous hope for you.

Even though there's nothing good within yourself that could ever make you right with God, and there is nothing you can do to work up enough righteousness to please God, He has sent His Son to die and take the punishment on Himself that we deserved. That's what the gospel is all about. It's good news. The good news is Christ can be your Savior from the wrath of God. *"For God so loved the world, that He gave His only begotten Son, that whoever believes in Him shall not perish, but have eternal life. For God did not send the Son into the world to judge the world, but that the world might be saved through Him." (John 3:16-17).* This is the good news, that Christ has come in the world, and He offers you salvation at this moment. But let me warn you, my reader, that Jesus is coming back a second time to the earth, an event called *the second coming of Christ.* And when He comes back, He's coming back to judge. So now is the time for salvation, not tomorrow and not in the future—but now!

> *"At the acceptable time I listened to you,*
> *And on the day of salvation I helped you."*
> *Behold, now is "the acceptable time," behold, now is "the*
> *day of salvation." (2 Corinthians 6:2)*

BLINDNESS

In all my years in talking to people who have lived troubled lives, one thing that always amazes me is their blindness when confronted with the truth of God's word upon their own lives. It's like seeing a man on fire and telling him, *"You're on fire, let me help."* He turns to you and says, *"No I'm not, I'm fine!"* That would be astonishing, wouldn't it? That's how it is many times, especially to family and friends of a troubled person. They have spoken to them many times, yet nothing seems to make sense to the troubled person, and with this comes the delusional effect that they actually think they are normal.

Truth is deflected from their understanding, so even commonsense ideas won't penetrate. Why? They are blind! Sin's natural fruit in a troubled person's life is spiritual blindness.

This is the judgment, that the Light has come into the world, and men loved the darkness rather than the Light, for their deeds were evil. For everyone who does evil hates the Light, and does not come to the Light for fear that his deeds will be exposed. But he who practices the truth comes to the Light, so that his deeds may be manifested as having been wrought in God. (John 3:19-21)

But a natural man does not accept the things of the Spirit of God, for they are foolishness to him; and he cannot understand them, because they are spiritually appraised. (1 Corinthians 2:14)

We have renounced the things hidden because of shame, not walking in craftiness or adulterating the word of God, but by the manifestation of truth commending ourselves to every man's conscience in the sight of God. And even if our gospel is veiled, it is veiled to those who are perishing, in whose case the god of this world5 has blinded the minds of the unbelieving so that they might not see the light of the gospel of the glory of Christ, who is the image of God. (2 Corinthians 4:2-4).

So this I say, and affirm together with the Lord, that you walk no longer just as the Gentiles also walk, in the futility

---

5 (Satan, the god of this world, is mentioned in this reference.)

of their mind, being darkened in their understanding, excluded from the life of God because of the ignorance that is in them, because of the hardness of their heart; and they, having become callous, have given themselves over to sensuality for the practice of every kind of impurity with greediness. (Ephesians 4:17-19)

There is what the Bible calls *spiritual blindness*, and this occurs to those who are lost, even those who think they're religious. Now why would God allow this? It may be that these kinds of people have been exposed to the gospel, heard the word of God, and know deep down in their hearts the right way to go. They have come to a point in their lives where truth can no longer penetrate their conscience and bring about repentance. But God who is rich in mercy always has His arms stretched out to welcome the prayer of a truly repentant person. He is a merciful and loving God who loves to forgive sin, through His Son, Jesus Christ. To this person He will grant eternal life with Him in glory, safe from His wrath, having given Him a new heart. Oh reader, this can be you. The time is not too late if you only realize who you really are, that you have been blind to the truth, making excuse after excuse for your sin. Will you make that choice today?

IDOL-WORSHIPERS

Most people, without realizing it, chase after things in their lives that become heart idols. Things like money, fame, sex, beauty or material possessions, when finally attained, always leave one feeling miserable, with the dreadful feeling of wanting more. These things never fully satisfy or bring true peace and contentment. These desires are no more than fruit of an evil heart. All of these things are idols of the heart, and by nature are always bent toward ones sinful nature. You may ask, *"What's a heart idol?"* It's anything in your life that stems from a selfish heart that mostly controls you. You love to do it even though it's sinful. Things like gambling, sinful sexual desires, drinking, fighting, doing drugs, the desire to gain more and more power or wealth, love and acceptance; all of these become very strong desires of the heart that you let supersede any desire to please God. And the only way to have the strength to overcome these things is through coming to salvation, experiencing the indwelling Spirit and the word of God. For the lost, it's as if they are naturally bent toward having idols in their life.

We might not bow down to a statue, but we have a lot of idols of the heart, and all these idols draw us away from God, just as Satan wants. If you were to honestly take an inventory of your desires, what you would find would be horrifying, especially since God knows everything about you anyway. Idols like greed, hatred, deceit, feeling that no one loves you anymore, are all selfish desires to please self. But when one truly comes to Christ, all these things dwindle and shift toward pleasing Christ and giving Him glory for all that you do, speak and think. That's the huge difference between a believer and one who is perhaps just a religious person. The difference is drastic, totally transforming one's desires and goals. For the lost, the focus is on self, pleasing self, feeling sorry for self and fulfilling self. But for those who come to Christ, dying to self and being resurrected to serve Him as a slave to Him, this is life with eternal promises, real hope, direction and joy in this life. The true focus of believers is on pleasing Christ in their lives and never doing anything to bring shame or dishonor to His name. That's the big difference, and that's the difference between you and a true believer. That's why I said if you were to take a true inventory of your life, you would probably see that everything revolves around what you need and want. Isn't it about time that you get real with yourself and come to terms with God your Creator—accepting His terms totally for your life and not your own. Consider what an Old Testament prophet named Ezekiel said about the lost who were very religious: *"Son of man, these men have set up their idols in their hearts and have put right before their faces the stumbling block of their iniquity. Should I be consulted by them at all?" (Ezekiel 14:3).*

Man has not changed much since then. People today still have idols of the heart, and if you truly want to please God and follow Him, you must repent of all these idols and give your full allegiance to Him.

A WRONG VIEW

Most people think of God as something like a lucky rabbit's foot, as one who is their co-pilot, someone to meet their inner or outer needs, or someone that will work with them if they do their part. Some also think that if they are good enough in life, He will bless them and let them into heaven because *"God is love,"* or He is *"the man upstairs"* that they think about once in a while at funerals or weddings. Others see Him as a *"higher power"* that guides them by a set of rules they themselves have created, their religion. Is He this kind of God? No He's not. He is not a God who is some kind of butler, waiting upon us so He can fulfill our dreams, desires and plans. Instead, He is the God of this universe, who created everything in it.

He is so pure and holy, so righteous in all His ways, that He fully deserves to have glory for Himself. In fact everything He does, even ordaining affliction and good, is all for His glory. He is God and He fully deserves to be glorified. So when you have a misinformed view about God and about truth, you will have an incorrect view of who God is, how He acts and what He expects of us. When bad things happen, because of a sinful lifestyle, people often automatically interpret things incorrectly about the events, even maybe blaming God Himself because of their problems. But the problems are much deeper than mere surface issue, for at the core is sin, and it's just that—your sin. God is not the author of sin, nor does He make anyone sin. People have chosen to live in their sin because it brings them many kinds of personal pleasures, even though those desires are evil. Unless they repent and turn to God for salvation and a true commitment to follow His word, their sin will consume and destroy them. People think it's bad now; their future looks very bleak!

> *These things you have done and I kept silence;*
> *You thought that I was just like you;*
> *I will reprove you and state the case in order before your*
> *eyes. (Psalm 50: 21)*

As I look about and grow older, I am saddened many times at the mass of people I see suffering and going through much agony in their lives. And to think that I know the ultimate cause (sin) and the solution (Christ and His word), that it can be frustrating when people reject this and choose to wallow in their trouble. But then I always come back to realize God has given us all a free will that gives us all the freedom to do so, even though so foolish!

A nature that won't "just change"

This is one area where people throughout the ages have had

the most difficulty with. Why? Because our natures are so infiltrated by sin, and because we desire to have total control of our lives, we lose sight of the truth and fail to realize the real truth about ourselves—a truth that is quite ugly. In desiring this, we then tend to shape God in a fashion that will meet those expectations. That's why idol-worship was so prevalent, and why it is still so today. People tend to create an image of "god" that functionally becomes their guidance throughout life. Creating for themselves a god who lets them get away with sin, one who won't be too judgmental. These kinds of gods will allow them to dwell in all their sinful ways and perhaps get a free pass to heaven. So they can have both idols of the heart, keeping to their own ways while still thinking they are going to heaven anyway because they merely *"believe in God."* The apostles John and Paul had much to say about this.

If we say that we have fellowship with Him and yet walk in the darkness, we lie and do not practice the truth; but if we walk in the Light as He Himself is in the Light, we have fellowship with one another, and the blood of Jesus His Son cleanses us from all sin. If we say that we have no sin, we are deceiving ourselves and the truth is not in us. If we confess our sins, He is faithful and righteous to forgive us our sins and to cleanse us from all unrighteousness. If we say that we have not sinned, we make Him a liar and His word is not in us. (1 John 1:6-10)

By this we know that we have come to know Him, if we keep His commandments. The one who says, "I have come to know Him," and does not keep His commandments, is a liar, and the truth is not in him; but whoever keeps His word, in him the love of God has truly been perfected. By this we know that we are in Him: the one who says he abides in Him ought himself to walk in the same manner as He walked. (1 John 2:3-5)

The one who says he is in the Light and yet hates his brother is in the darkness until now. The one who loves his brother abides in the Light and there is no cause for stumbling in him. But the one who hates his brother is in the darkness and walks in the darkness, and does not know where he is going because the darkness has blinded his eyes. (1 John 2:9-11)

Do not love the world nor the things in the world. If anyone loves the world, the love of the Father is not in him. For all that is in the world, the lust of the flesh and the lust of the eyes and the boastful pride of life, is not from the Father, but is from the world. The world is passing away, and also its lusts; but the one who does the will of God lives forever. (1 John 2:15-17)

Little children, make sure no one deceives you; the one who practices righteousness is righteous, just as He is righteous; the one who practices sin is of the devil; for the devil has sinned from the beginning. The Son of God appeared for this purpose, to destroy the works of the devil. No one who is born of God practices sin, because His seed abides in him; and he cannot sin, because he is born of God. By this the children of God and the children of the devil are obvious: anyone who does not practice righteousness is not of God, nor the one who does not love his brother.
(1 John 3:7-10)

Not only are we incapable of attaining righteousness, we are totally incapable of saving ourselves. This is where Maria was in her life and thinking. There can be no worse a plight than a religious person who spends his whole life thinking he is going to heaven, but ends up in hell after dying. Most fail to understand their standing before a Holy God.

...for all have sinned and fall short of the glory of God, being justified as a gift by His grace through the redemption which is in Christ Jesus... (Romans 3:23-24).

For by grace you have been saved through faith; and that not of yourselves, it is the gift of God; not as a result of works, so that no one may boast. For we are His workmanship, created in Christ Jesus for good works, which God prepared beforehand so that we would walk in them. (Ephesians 2:8-10)

[God] has saved us and called us with a holy calling, not according to our works, but according to His own purpose and grace which was granted us in Christ Jesus from all eternity... (2 Timothy 1:9)

For the grace of God has appeared, bringing salvation to all men, instructing us to deny ungodliness and worldly desires and to live sensibly, righteously and godly in the present age, looking for the blessed hope and the appearing of the glory of our great God and Savior, Christ Jesus, who gave Himself for us to redeem us from every lawless deed, and to purify for Himself a people for His own possession, zealous for good deeds. (Titus 2:11-14)

You must realize that if you really desire to change, all that you do and all the good deeds you have done in the past can never be good enough to change a sinful heart. It is only through the power of the Holy Spirit who comes in to dwell in your life at salvation, that it becomes possible to change your stony heart to a soft heart, all done by the power of God. The presence of the Holy Spirit in your life gives you the power and ability to carry out the word of God. That is the key to change. There is nothing you can do; you are incapable and totally powerless to bring about this change—the new birth—that is so desperately needed. It is only by the work of God that this can be accomplished when you come to Him repentant, sincerely seeking His salvation and with a pure heart that desires His daily presence. You have to be willing to humble yourself, and become a slave for Christ. What God desires is for you to realize that you are fully and completely a sinner. If you were to die tonight and stand before Him, He would have to judge you as not of His fold. But He wants to save your soul because He loves you. Do you really love Him? I must emphasize that people like Maria are totally powerless to change, as the rest of us are, and that's why God has to use His grace to shed upon our useless and dead souls. You are helpless, yet He is willing.

SHORTSIGHTEDNESS

People have a natural tendency to take this short life span of some seventy to eighty years on average, and selfishly use it all up on themselves, choosing to greedily grasp on to these short years while passing up endless billions of years in total bliss, happiness, joy and true fulfillment on a new earth with God and all the other people who have chosen to follow the Lord Jesus (see Revelation 21). Why would anyone make such a poor choice? Because they want to seek their own desires and glory rather than God's. The Bible calls them fools. A sinful person seeks to please self before anyone else, even God. Foolish people do foolish things! As I've counseled people who lived troubled lives, one of the common threads is that they are usually very short-sighted in their perspective on life. What I mean by this is their focus in life is so much on themselves that they rarely think of pleasing God. They perhaps want a relationship with Him, but on their terms rather than His. But He is too great, too glorious and too deserving to ever bend the knee to any human being's sinful desires. If anyone needs to bend their knees, we are the ones. The troubled person's view on life is usually very twisted. What needs to occur is a broadening of their perspective on eternity. God said there are only two places to spend eternity—heaven or hell. He desires for the troubled person to repent and come to Him for salvation, and this is true and eternal salvation now and forever. But the troubled person is so focused on his daily troubles and desires, that he loses the big picture. He fails to take seriously all the repercussions of his sinful actions and thoughts toward God and others.

On the other hand, true believers see the big picture and when things come along in life that are hard and affliction follows, they have a hope through it all because of the big picture God has given us. This life is not all there is. There's much more to life than just today. A true believer's goal is to bring glory to God and have a desire to do that in eternity. In other words, true believers desire to lead selfless lives, seeking to minister to others the good news of the gospel, and using their lives to help other believers. It is a totally opposite from a self-centered life to an others' oriented kind of life. And that's exactly why the troubled person is so lost and alone. Whenever people turn inward on themselves and seek to please themselves every day, all they heap up for themselves is eternal destruction for their souls in hell and misery to others. Things won't get better, only worse. Any time a person turns fully inward, an implosion will occur eventually in the person's life, causing misery, emptiness and a loss of life direction.

FORGIVENESS

On the average, people want forgiveness for themselves when they do wrong but when it is reversed, it is rare for them to offer forgiveness. Usually revenge, an avenging spirit, hate or bitterness is incorporated into the person's actions. We are so bent on doing this that it keeps our courts and jails full, creating lives filled with depression, failures, and suicides by the thousands. This is also one of the major aspects of a prodigal's life. It is usually filled with some kind of lack of forgiveness and bitterness in the past or near present, that it fills the mind, indulging the minds as if it will never leave; almost like a dead man's body attached to a person's back, inescapably present.

Yet this is so different from God and His ways. He is a forgiving God, willing to forgive even the vilest offender if that person comes to Him repentant, willing to follow Him.

For You, Lord, are good, and ready to forgive,
And abundant in lovingkindness to all who call upon You.
(Psalm 86:5)

For He rescued us from the domain of darkness, and trans-
ferred us to the kingdom of His beloved Son, in whom we
have redemption, the forgiveness of sins.
(Colossians 1:13-14)

54

In that God forgives us, He in return asks those who follow Him to do likewise—to be forgiving. A person who is a forgiving person is one who will be at peace with himself and with the Lord. In fact, God commands us to live this way.

Be kind to one another, tender-hearted, forgiving each other, just as God in Christ also has forgiven you. (Ephesians 4:32)

God has also said that if we fail to forgive others, God in turn will not forgive us, and that's a serious issue! But if we learn to forgive, there is a certain kind of freedom and peace of heart we can have in our lives. But if we chose to do the opposite, much bitterness will stay in our lives, causing many issues to occur. Anyone who does this will have his thinking constantly dwelling on things that are ever so burdensome; in fact, it can be captivating at times, even to the point that it becomes an ever present issue of self talk.

APPLICATION PROJECTS: WEEK #1

Each reading for the week will end with some simple personal application projects that will help you in your life. The important thing about this homework is this: are you willing to be honest and open about yourself? If you can, look at yourself objectively, look at who you are, how you live and why you do things.

1 According to today's lesson, what are some of Maria's problems?

....

....

....

....

2 We discussed Romans 1:24 and how God gives some people up to their sin. What does all that mean according to today's lesson?

....

....

....

....

3 According to what you read today, does just believing in God mean you're a true Christian? Explain why or why not.

....

....

....

....

4 In light of today's lesson, write a few things about how God views us as humans.

....

....

....

....

5 In this lesson, we talked a lot about the fruit of our lives. Below, I want you to do something that may be hard. If you're serious about changing and pleasing God, be honest. Think about how you have lived during the past few days. What were some of your life fruits? Check off the things you did, either in your heart or outwardly toward others. But realize that many things we do start from the heart and even though no one else knows what you may have done, God does. And remember, this list is just between you and God.

☐ I lied.

☐ I was selfish.

☐ I committed sexual immorality.

☐ I deceived someone by not telling the real truth.

☐ I fought with someone.

☐ Had bitter thoughts against someone.

☐ I lusted after someone sexually.

☐ I felt sorry for myself.

☐ I got angry.

☐ I was greedy with my money.

☐ I stole something that really wasn't mine; perhaps at work, home, or market.

☐ I got jealous of someone else.

☐ I used drugs or alcohol to get high.

☐ I gambled away money that should have been used for other responsible things.

☐ I spoke meanly to somebody.

☐ I broke the law.

☐ Write out something you may have done wrong that is not listed here.

6 If you are honest in the way you have responded in the list above, you have taken a big step toward change. As you look at this list, you may have known all along that you walked in the flesh, and brought forth the fruit of the flesh. This list may reveal the true you, the way you really are, and something God already knew about you. In the verses below, look them up in your Bible and write out what they are teaching.

Galatians 5:19-21

....

....

....

Galatians 5:22-26

....

....

....

Ephesians 2:1-3

....

....

....

Ephesians 2:4-10

....

....

....

Romans 13:11-14

....

....

....

....

Romans 7:5

....

....

....

7 Memorize Ephesians 2:8-9.

2

God's View of the Right Solution

WEEK TWO

Now that we know how God views the entire human race, how in the world could we ever be assured of our eternal future? Think about this. We are basically evil, so even our good works are like filthy rags to Him (see Isaiah 64:6). We can never earn our way to heaven through doing good works or by leading good lives. If we do not have the Spirit of God indwelling us and are not living in obedience to God's Word, what hope can we have? I know people always try to create their own means and own beliefs about all this.

Someone may say that you are worth something to God or that you can earn your way to heaven by performing good works. These sayings have been around for thousands of years. But the real question is, "What about God?" What has He said? Can people create their own ideas and doctrines and somehow slip past God in all this? Can they create their own bliss and have the ability to live forever? Can't a brilliant person with extraordinary talent, genius or power create his own reality that will muster up enough means to have it work? The answer is "NO." Since God does exist and has spoken, then nothing in the entire physical or spiritual realms could supersede His plans. We all must face it. We all live in a moral universe in which all are accountable before a moral God who says one day we will all stand before Him and give an account of our lives.

THE BAD NEWS FIRST

If you listen today to talk about what a Christian is, great emphasis is placed on God's love, mercy, and forgiveness, and how a loving God wouldn't send a good person to hell. You may even believe this yourself. Easy-believeism is everywhere today. "Accept Jesus in your heart," people proclaim, but with little emphasis on the importance of a changed life. It's as though this new message emphasizes a devilish lie—that you can keep your sin and have God, too. Is this really what the Bible teaches? No it's not. In fact, it's quite the opposite. Have you ever heard of "the law of God"?

As you read the Bible, the law of God is everywhere, and it's not good news for the human race, for it describes both the very nature of God and His standard for each of us. The law is a reflection of God's nature, His holiness, purity and His standards for us. The law is perfect, holy and good because it is a mirror of God's divine nature. The law was set down in the Ten Commandments (Exodus 20) and Jesus revealed that God's law is not only defined by external behavior but is always a heart issue and that we are held responsible as well to God's law (Matthew 5-7). When He preached the Sermon on the Mount, He revealed that standard again as to the life of a true Christian. The religious leaders of His day had watered down the law to such an extent that it became nothing more than mere external religious behaviors and because of this they were actually saying they kept the whole law of God when, in reality, Jesus judged them as lost, hypocritical and deserving of hell for leading others astray as well. It ultimately was a heart issue, one that relates to one's motives before a Holy God and His standards. Anyone who breaks one of these laws is guilty of them all and deserves hell. The standard was set for us by God Himself.

Therefore you are to be perfect, as your heavenly Father is perfect. (Matthew 5:48)

This is the standard set down by God; you must be perfect, never sinning once in your entire life. And to make things even worse, the law doesn't save. It offers no other way of salvation, and it offers no hope or forgiveness. Galatians 3 testifies to this. The law of God is the very standard set up by God to judge us as to our standing before Him, and it condemns us all. That's why it's bad news for us because it condemns everybody ever born. It condemns me and you!

Cursed is everyone who does not continue in all things which are written in the law, to do them. (Galatians 3:10)

We are all under the curse of sin because no one keeps it all perfectly. That's why Paul says in Galatians 3:11, *"Now that no one is justified by the Law before God is evident."* All are condemned because we all broke the law. So why would God give us the law? Look at Galatians 3:19—a question that asks, in effect, *"What purpose does the law serve?"* The law reveals to us not only God's divine nature of perfection, but it reveals man's utter sinfulness and inability to save himself by good works. This is what Paul meant in Ephesians 2: 8-9. No one can work good deeds and earn a passage to heaven. The law has already condemned us and we all stand condemned—you, I, and the whole human race. There are several things about the law that affect us all.

- The law of God requires our lives to be a certain way that is opposite to the way we really live. Instead, we know our hearts are selfish, self-indulgent, desiring sinful things and that they love sin.
- The law of God requires us to live perfect lives, yet it's impossible to reach that goal because of sin. "because the mind set on the flesh is hostile toward God; for it does not subject itself to the law of God, for it is not even able to do so" (Romans 8:7).
- The law of God expects us to be perfect and accepts nothing less. We can never meet that standard.
- The law of God never accepts half-way attempts, as if we

64

could try our best and that would be good enough. No. It's either total perfection throughout all our lives or nothing.

- The law of God accepts no limited payments, certain ritualistic performances, good deeds or sacrifices as a way of satisfying God's demand for perfection. It promises damnation if anyone violates even one of its laws.
- The law of God never eases up or lightens the load as to God's requirements. It has maintained, and always will maintain, that you have to be perfect to be a saved from the wrath of God.
- The law of God looks at all humans ever born and condemns them as guilty, deserving hell. This brings dread, fear and shame.
- The law of God deliverers to people a very severe sentence, eternal separation from Him, and eternal damnation in hell.
- The law itself provides no help, no strength, and no power to save us. It cannot help the sinner.
- When we break the law, it offers no path back to God for salvation. It doesn't offer any way back at all.
- The law of God listens to no repentance, no sorrows, and no cries. It compares your life to itself and condemns, shutting the door to any hope.
- In the law of God there is no forgiveness, there are no deeds good enough to accept, no repentance, and no forgetting or putting behind.
- The law actually stirs up sin in our lives, making us aware of what we should be doing but, because of our sinful desires, we want to do the opposite.
- The law of God offers no pronouncement of a better day or hope for the future. It just condemns us. The sentence is to eternal damnation.

As you read about the law of God, it's pretty bleak. And

that's where you stand now perhaps. God knows that you have broken His law and you stand condemned before Him as one deserving eternal separation. God, being a righteous judge, must judge everyone as guilty. But there is hope. Look back at the question of Galatians 3:19—what was the purpose of the law? *"It was added because of transgressions, having been ordained through angels by the agency of a mediator, until the seed would come to whom the promise had been made."* The law was given and condemns the whole human race until the seed comes? Who is the seed and what can it do to save us from the law? Look at verse 16, *"The seed is Christ."* The law leads us to Christ—our only hope.

As you read the Old Testament, running alongside the law was the sacrificial system. Thousands of animals were killed to show us that a sacrifice had to be made to deal with our sins and the law's condemnation of it before a holy and just God. Something great had to be done to deliver us from the law that condemns us. Christ is that one who lived the perfect life without ever breaking one of God's laws; He would be a perfect sacrifice for our sins, in our place. He would come and take the punishment we deserved, because of the law, and God would see this perfect sacrifice and remove His wrath from over our heads. Because Christ lived a perfect life, he could say, "I have come to fulfill the law" (see Matthew 5:17).

Christ lived a perfect life and completely pleased God. He never did anything wrong, never sinned, never broke one of God's laws in his entire life and because of this He could be the perfect sacrifice that God demanded for our sins. *"For by one offering He has perfected for all time those who are sanctified."* *(Hebrews 10:14).* The word sanctified means "to make holy or to set apart." When Christ fulfilled the will of God, He provided for the believer a continuing and permanent condition of being saved from the law's condemnation and the wrath of God. Realizing there is absolutely nothing they could do to earn their salvation, either by good deeds or sacrifices, they can run to Christ their Savior. That's why Christ is called our Savior. Savior from what? From God sin and from the righteous judgments of a Holy God. You are lost in your sins and you need Christ to save you! You have nothing to offer, no good deeds or works. There is absolutely nothing within yourself to offer Him. Your part is to realize you are helpless before the law, that you are a sinner, but that God has opened the way of forgiveness. That way is through faith—faith in Christ as both your Savior and Lord/Master.

For by grace you have been saved through faith, and that not of yourselves. (Ephesians 2:8)

It was God who gave us the law to show both His holy nature and standard by which He will judge. But it is by God's mercy and love that He offers grace to those only who are willing to come under the complete lordship of Christ, putting their complete faith in Him and His work on the cross on their behalf. Because Christ was perfect, He had no sins to atone for. But because of His great love for sinners like you, He willingly walked forward and let evil men beat, spit, and curse and crucify Him and, most of all, take the punishment that you deserved from God and placed all that upon Himself. And in doing this God was well pleased and accepted His Son's offering on your behalf. To all those who were willing to die to self and be raised to serve Christ as their Master and Lord, willing to put their faith in Him, to these the judgment of God has been removed and forgiveness is spread abroad in their hearts.

That's why the term *"The Gospel"* is good news. The law was bad news but the good news is about salvation through faith in Christ.

THE GOOD NEWS

So what is the right solution? Jesus and His work on the Cross on your behalf. But don't get me wrong here. It's not necessarily a one-time decision that you may have made in the past, the signing of a card, a raising of the hand or a child baptism, as if you could buy life or fire insurance for the future against hell.

It is the most serious commitment for life you will ever make because Jesus said you must die to selfish desires, take up your cross daily, and follow Him. What Jesus demands for Himself is all of you and all of your life or nothing. Why? Because you're worth nothing, you can offer nothing, and you are totally powerless. But God's great love and mercy is ready to be shed upon your life. And the solution is what Christ did on the cross. He suffered much while on this earth so a path of salvation could be opened to those who desired it. It may be helpful for the troubled person to realize who Jesus is and what He did on your behalf. Let's take a quick look at all of this and see what Jesus did and how he suffered for you.

If you could pick the one person in all of human history who has suffered the most, who would you choose? Some may say Adam, the first person who ever lived. But he is not the one. True, it is Adam who, of all humans in history, brought the most afflictions upon us all. Because of his decision to rebel, he plunged the entire human race and all of creation into trials, hardships and death.

Still others may say it was Job. Surely he was innocent and suffered much at the hands of Satan. He lost all his children, his farm, and his animals. He suffered with boils all over his body and he sat in ashes. But again the answer is no. He was not the one who suffered the most. How about Paul the Apostle? At one time he had power, prestige, and a high position as a Pharisee but once he had become a follower of Christ, He saw all those honors as dung. He chose to follow Christ and, because of this, he suffered many beatings, imprisonments, shipwrecks, abandonment by friends and family, and ended up being executed. Surely he suffered the most? No, not the most. Who is this one person if there ever was one?

Let me paint for you a true picture of this person before giving you their name. Suppose you were the type of person who lived a totally innocent life. You never hurt anyone, never said anything wrong against anyone, you followed God's Word in all you did and, most of all (which is the most unique thing), you always put others before yourself. Now that's unique! Why is this one person so different? Because every human ever born is stamped with the idea that they are the center of the universe and that people were made to serve them, to meet their needs, and that selfishness comes more easily than breathing itself.

You're probably wondering who this person is. His name is Jesus. He suffered more than any human ever born—and not just physical abuse. Yes, He suffered great afflictions at a young age, He was treated terribly, beaten and hung on a cross where He died, but so did thousands of others of His time. Following Him, all his disciples suffered great afflictions and were murdered, except one—the Apostle John, who was exiled on a prison island. So what makes Jesus so unique? Why are His sufferings different than all the millions throughout history who suffered greatly and died? The place to go for all our facts is the Holy Scripture. I will outline who

69

Jesus was and why He suffered so much so that, when we are finished, it will be clear that He was truly unique in His sufferings.

He lived before He was born
This may sound strange but it is true. He lived even before the physical universe was brought into existence.

> *"I will surely tell of the decree of the LORD:*
> *He said to Me, 'You are My Son,*
> *Today I have begotten You.*
> *'Ask of Me, and I will surely give the nations as Your inheritance,*
> *And the very ends of the earth as Your possession."*
> *(Psalm 2:7-8)*

This verse is discussing the Messiah and is the Old Testament reference to the Father-Son relationship within the Trinity, which was planned in eternity past and fully realized in the incarnation of Jesus on the earth. This verse is quoted in the New Testament with reference to His birth (Hebrews 1:5-6), and also to His resurrection (Acts 13:33-34) as the ultimate fulfillment.

> *Jesus said to them, "Truly, truly, I say to you, before Abraham was born, I am." (John 8:58)*

Jesus existed before the world began. He affirmed this before creation while preaching to His disciples, the common people and religious leaders. Jesus started off His amazing address in John's Gospel, Chapter 8, with the words *"most assuredly"* (New King James Version). Jesus used this phrase to emphasize the importance and vital truth of what He is about to say. Then He shocks them all by saying *"I AM"* (the underlying Greek phrase, *"ego eimi,"* is emphatic). Here Jesus declared Himself to be God (*Jehovah* or *Yahweh* as it is sometimes rendered), the LORD referred to throughout the Old Testament. This was a basic statement used of God as in Exodus 3:14; Deuteronomy 32:39; Isaiah 41:4 and 43:10. In all these passages God declared Himself preexistent and eternal— without beginning and without end. The people hearing Jesus say these things were not mistaken as to what He meant. That's why they took up stones to kill Him (verse 59). Jesus used this statement twenty-three times in all (4:26;6:20;35;41;48;51; 8:12; 18;24;28;58; 10:7;9;11;14; 11:25; 13:19; 14:6; 15:1; 5; 18:5;6;8). Jesus made it very clear that He lived before everyone else.

> *He is the image of the invisible God, the firstborn of all creation. For by Him all things were created, both in the heavens and on earth, visible and invisible, whether thrones or dominions or rulers or authorities—all things have been created through Him and for Him. (Colossians 1:15-16)*

His preexistence was also proclaimed by the apostles. They knew well enough that He was God and existed before creation itself. The Greek word for image is *"eikon"* and it means "an exact copy or likeness." Jesus is the perfect image or exact likeness of the God of heaven (Philippians 2:6; John 1:14; 14:9). He has always been this way and will continue for eternity. These verses also teach that Jesus created both the visible and invisible things—and that's the spiritual and physical creation. He created it all for Himself. Only God could do this.

71

MISSION? WORLD!

You have to grasp this to really understand why He suffered more than anyone else in all of time. He is God. He created everything that exists, in both the spiritual and physical worlds. He has the ability to live for eternity. He is the most powerful being in all creation and His powers are incomprehensible, along with His intricate will for human history. But at the exact time planned by the Trinity, He came to earth and allowed Himself to become a human child, born of a woman, in a poor, dirty and cold manger, a place where animals ate—God in a manger, that's an astonishing thing! The Creator and God of everything was in a manger! He was not obligated to come here to earth or obligated to do anything at all to this rebellious human race. But out of His deep and abiding love, and because of our election before time began, He chose to do these things. This act alone shows His otherness, His being above and beyond comprehension for the acts He performs—something we humans could not and would not do for others. It was predicted by Isaiah the prophet eight hundred years before it even occurred.

> *Therefore the Lord Himself will give you a sign: Behold, a virgin will be with child and bear a son, and she will call His name Immanuel. (Isaiah 7:14)*

The term Immanuel means *"God with us"* and is applied to Jesus Himself in Matthew 1:23. God, the creator of all you see and don't see, was with human beings, the very ones He created. God, the One who rules the universe and human events in all of time, was with them. What an astounding reality!

Some people may say, *"If only Jesus came today instead,*

things would have been so different". This isn't true. Society would still reject Him and somehow arrange to have Him executed as He was 2,000 years ago. But it has to be mentioned that God never makes mistakes. Jesus, by His own will and love, came to earth at exactly the right time, to the right people, in the right country, at the right place, to start His work of such a great redemption, just as the Trinity planned before creation came into being.

> *But when the fullness of the time came, God sent forth His Son, born of a woman, born under the Law, so that He might redeem those who were under the Law, that we might receive the adoption as sons. (Galatians 4:4-5)*

> *But we do see Him who was made for a little while lower than the angels, namely, Jesus, because of the suffering of death crowned with glory and honor, so that by the grace of God He might taste death for everyone. (Hebrews 2:9)*

The Creator afflicted by His creation

There were several things Jesus came to do here on this earth that were specific in nature. The first was to do the will of His Father in heaven. The Trinity, before creation, had already planned for the Messiah to come to the earth. Thus Jesus fulfills that plan. In John's Gospel, Jesus spoke these words:

> *For I have come down from heaven, not to do My own will, but the will of Him who sent Me. This is the will of Him who sent Me, that of all that He has given Me I lose nothing, but raise it up on the last day. For this is the will of My Father, that everyone who beholds the Son and believes in Him will have eternal life, and I Myself will raise him up on the last*

day." (John 6:38-40)

That was an awesome mission. To save a people of such rebellious hearts takes a great mercy and love. Jesus came to save sinners. The term *"sinners"* is a way of saying that every human ever born is a person who is bent on sinning. People habitually walk in rebellion against God. It takes little effort to sin, as it all comes so naturally. Thus, they are sinners, sinning all the time. It is to such people that God the Son goes into dangerous trenches to save. But to save them from what? God! God is a loving and merciful God but, because He is totally righteous in all His ways, He also has to be righteous—a just judge. Therefore He has to judge sin. For the human population this is bad. Because we are all sinners by nature, we are all, by nature, doomed to eternity, away from God, heaven and eternal bliss. But God Himself came to earth to be spit upon, beaten, whipped and killed by those He came to save. That is a travesty beyond measure. But He, being God, knew this was going to happen and yet still He came.

> *He was despised and forsaken of men,*
> *A man of sorrows and acquainted with grief;*
> *And like one from whom men hide their face*
> *He was despised, and we did not esteem Him.*
> *Surely our griefs He Himself bore,*
> *And our sorrows He carried;*
> *Yet we ourselves esteemed Him stricken,*
> *Smitten of God, and afflicted.*
> *But He was pierced through for our transgressions,*
> *He was crushed for our iniquities;*
> *The chastening for our well-being fell upon Him,*
> *And by His scourging we are healed. (Isaiah 53:3-5)*

Jesus, although God in the flesh, suffered on the cross and was imputed with the wrath of God the Father that we deserved for our sin. God laid this on the Son at the cross. There He suffered for the sins of people who would believe. God then imputes His righteousness to us, giving us eternal life with Him. That is incredible! He suffered for us even though He was innocent, so that we, who rebelled, could spend eternity with Him. Not a fair trade at all from a human perspective, but one in which only God could do through His awesome grace and mercy. This is such a great love that we, while alive here on earth, could never fully grasp. But once we are in eternity, our spiritual eyes will be fully opened and at the reality of all this we will naturally fall to our knees in worship. Then we will understand this great work of God on our behalf and the great cost it was for God the Son. That is real love! In this act of sacrifice He can now offer real, eternal life to those who believe in His sacrificial work. And in all this we have the supreme example we believers are to have toward God and others, a sacrificial lifestyle.

The thief comes only to steal and kill and destroy; I came that they may have life, and have it abundantly.
(John 10:10)

In these verses, Jesus is insisting, as God, that belief in Him as the Messiah and the Son of God is the only way of being saved from sin and hell and instead receiving eternal life. It should also be mentioned that it was in God's plan to have the Messiah suffer affliction according to Scripture. Study the following verses: Psalm 22; Isaiah 53; Matthew 16:21, Mark 8:31; Luke 9:22; 17:25; 18:31-33; 24:25-26; Acts 8:31. Before time itself was created, Jesus knew He would suffer greatly so that people like you could spend eternity with Him. This is why He is the one person who has suffered the most in all human history. He was not obligated to come down from heaven; He had the power at any time to deal out retribution and the authority to stop such injustice against Him, but instead took the beatings, cursing, spitting and death, even though He was the most innocent man. In this He chose to die like a lamb, quiet and meek, before the slaughterers. But when He comes back the second time, His arrival will be dramatically different, in that He will bring suffering with Him. It is all about judgment and affliction upon those living on the earth. It will be a blessing to the elect but affliction such as has never been seen in human history (Luke 17:22-37). It will be days of carnage and death.

Buy and prayerfully read John MacArthur's book, *The Keys to Spiritual Growth* (Wheaton, Ill.: Crossway Books, 2001).

APPLICATION PROJECTS: WEEK #2

1 According to the reading, why was the law given?

....

....

....

2 Is there anything you can do to appease God for your sin? Why or why not?

....

....

....

3 What was God's solution to your sin problem?

....

....

....

4 In your understanding, what is faith?

....

....

....

5 By referring to the Bible, state who Jesus is and why He came to earth.

....

....

....

6 After this reading, in what areas of your daily life have you been rebellious?

....

....

....

7 Memorize Matthew 16:24-26.

3

Facing Who You Really Are before God

WEEK THREE

JESUS AS MASTER

Today, many people call themselves *"Christian."* And there seems to be all kinds of Christians as you look around. Turn on the TV and the picture you see is a happy, self-willed, wealthy and healthy person whose life is dictated by God meeting his or her every whim. Some people have come to the point where they themselves actually define what it means to be a Christian. To such people, He is our pal, our buddy, a god whose goal it is to satisfy all our desires. We are told that He is also a god who has become much more merciful than He was in the Old Testament times and doesn't take sin as a serious matter anymore—that if you name it, claim it, visualize it, it will come about. Is this the God of the Bible?

This may come as a shock but, no, He's not, even though we are given this kind of picture from many pulpits and big screen TVs. He is not our personal buddy, our pal, and definitely not our waiter, standing by to please our selfish desires. Instead He is Lord, Master and God of all creation who has laid out in Scripture what a true believer looks like, and that's what I'm about to challenge you with now. You are about to delve into something that may reveal the ugliness of your sin and lack of true salvation. It won't be easy and it definitely goes against what you may hear and see today. So let's consider the Bible and see what God's definition of a true Christian is. Let's start off by looking in John 13:12-13 where Jesus clearly says He is Lord.

> He said to them, "Do you know what I have done to you? You call Me Teacher and Lord; and you are right, for so I am."

Here Jesus calls Himself Lord. The Greek word is *"kurios"* and carries the idea of one who has power, absolute authority,

80

and a total right to control. It's a very powerful term, used of Him being God, Master of all. In fact, this word is used 747 times in the New Testament. This concept has largely been set aside in modern definitions of Christianity to the extent that He is diminished to the level of a servant awaiting our slightest commands. But this definition is the opposite of God's view. Jude warns us about people who watered down the lordship of Christ.

> *For certain persons have crept in unnoticed, those who were long beforehand marked out for this condemnation, ungodly persons who turn the grace of our God into licentiousness and deny our only Master and Lord, Jesus Christ. (Jude 4)*
>
> *But false prophets also arose among the people, just as there will also be false teachers among you, who will secretly introduce destructive heresies, even denying the Master who bought them, bringing swift destruction upon themselves. (2 Peter 2:1)*

Since Jesus is Master, that means he has slaves. During the time that Jesus used this terminology, slavery was a norm, fully accepted and acceptable. Jesus didn't condemn it, nor did the apostles, and neither did He condone it. But He borrowed this living metaphor to picture in the mind of those who wanted to follow Him what it would require. A master is not a master unless he has a slave—that's obvious. If Jesus is Master, who would His slaves be? Those who desired to become a slave of Christ. Since the people of Jesus' time were fully immersed in slavery and all the words used to describe it, is it a surprise we see so much of it being used as a picture of a true Christians? We are slaves and He is the Master. That's the imagery Jesus wanted to convey to His true followers.

So what does a slave look like? He or she has no rights, no options to be obedient or not. Whatever the master says, the slave does. That's why Jesus' words caused many who heard Him to walk away; they knew exactly what He was talking about. His often-repeated sayings like *"Take up your cross and follow Me"* resounded with a sense of the importance of obedience (Luke 9:23).

Let's now take a tour through the Bible and see what it means to be a slave of Christ. But let me warn you here because most translations today shy away from the word *slave* because of its negative connotations and instead translates the word *doulos* (slave) to *servant or bondslave*. However, we are not servants. Servants have options, they get paid, they can choose to work for their master or not, and can leave to go back home after their work. Instead, by biblical contrast, we actually are slaves!

> *...that if you confess with your mouth Jesus as Lord, and believe in your heart that God raised Him from the dead, you will be saved... (Romans 10:9)*

These are powerful words. You have to confess from your heart that Jesus is your Master and Lord, which automatically means you are willing to become His slave, willing to be obedient to His desires and even die for Him. We are asked to give up our own personal dreams, ambitions and submit ourselves to an alien will. For twenty-first-century Americans and other westerners, this is a hard concept to accept. But in Jesus' times it was fully understood by those around Him. The Old Testament saints knew this well (Acts 2:18), the apostles knew it (Acts 4:28-29), and the demons even knew they were slaves (Acts 16:17). Pastors and elders of the church knew they were slaves (Colossians 4:7, 2 Timothy 2:24). Even the Apostle John, writing about the future, knew there would be slaves of Christ in heaven (Revelation 1:1; 7:3; 10:7; 19:2). At the end of time, when all the future judgments have occurred, we will be slaves of God, serving Him forever (Revelation 22:3, 6). Paul the Apostle saw himself as a slave (Romans 1:1), as did James (James 1:1), Peter (2 Peter 1:1), Jude (Jude 1) and John the Apostle (Revelation 1:1).

But this picture becomes even more developed for the true believer. The Scriptures say *"We were chosen"* (see Ephesians 4:1). It pictures a master going into the market place and buying a slave or two from among the many. This is the picture of believers chosen by Christ before the foundation of the world. The Master had, however, to pay a price. What price was God willing to pay for His elect, chosen slaves that would serve Him? His own life. In fact, Jesus was willing to become a slave Himself on behalf of people like you. Consider what Paul says about this:

Have this attitude in yourselves which was also in Christ Jesus, who, although He existed in the form of God, did not regard equality with God a thing to be grasped, but emptied Himself, taking the form of a bond-servant, and being made in the likeness of men. Being found in appearance as a man, He humbled Himself by becoming obedient to the point of death, even death on a cross. (Philippians 2:5-8)

So even our Master became a slave of obedience to the Father, even unto death. This is what makes a true Christian— obedience to the Master. Masters command, we obey (read

John 15:10, 12, 14, 17). But Jesus goes one step further: He calls us *friends*. We are slaves, but we are intimately close to our Master because He has revealed to us His will. In biblical terms, anyone who is a true Christian lovingly and willingly obeys Christ and what He commands.

If you keep My commandments, you will abide in My love; just as I have kept My Father's commandments and abide in His love. (John 15:10)

You are My friends if you do what I command you. (John 15:14)

For who has known the mind of the Lord, that he will instruct Him? But we have the mind of Christ. (1 Corinthians 2:16)

For us as slaves, God has revealed what He desires (John 15:14-16). In Jesus' day, this concept of a slave being a friend of the master was very rare. It was reserved only for slaves that were very close to the master and knew what he wanted and desired. They were called his friends because he revealed to them his will. Today, we have the wholly known counsel of God, the Bible, revealing to us the mind of the Master to His slaves—and those slaves who are themselves His friends. And His slaves are known for their obedience. And as in the case of a slave, the Master fully expects us to be obedient to His word, which is why He has given the Spirit to dwell within us, giving us the ability to carry out His will. Read Luke 17:7-10 to get a picture of this.

There is a close relative of mine who claims that he is a Christian, but when one looks at his lifestyle, there is a big divide. He lies and deceives when it's convenient; he's irresponsible with his money through gambling. He's selfish, self-centered, refuses to work and has little desire to put Christ first. Basically we all have one of two spiritual mentors that we will reflect in our lives. Either it's Christ and our lives reflect Him, or it's Satan, and our lives will reflect this. Lies, deceit, selfishness and no desire to bring glory to God but to self, that's a lost sinner whose father is Satan. My relative, even though claiming Christ verbally to others, has a life that reflects his true spiritual father, Satan and his characteristics, and not those of Christ.

One may make many claims to be a true believer, but unless that person sees himself as a lost sinner before a God who will hold him accountable for all he does, comes to Him, asking for His mercy and salvation through Christ (even though realizing he deserves hell.) In coming to Him, that person is forgiven through Christ's sacrifice on the cross and is truly born again, regenerated, becoming a changed person. For this person, his desire now is to please Christ in all he does and he is willing to become a slave of Him who bought him from the slave-market of sin.

> *Therefore, prepare your minds for action, keep sober in spirit, fix your hope completely on the grace to be brought to you at the revelation of Jesus Christ. As obedient children, do not be conformed to the former lusts which were yours in your ignorance, but like the Holy One who called you, be holy yourselves also in all your behavior... (1 Peter 1:13-15)*

As believers, our view of Lordship isn't shaped by our own personal views or wills but instead by the Master who bought us, even with His own blood. We are to be under total submission to our Lord and Master. That's why Jesus said repeatedly:

Then Jesus said to His disciples, "If anyone wishes to come after Me, he must deny himself, and take up his cross and follow Me. For whoever wishes to save his life will lose it; but whoever loses his life for My sake will find it. For what will it profit a man if he gains the whole world and forfeits his soul? Or what will a man give in exchange for his soul? For the Son of Man is going to come in the glory of His Father with His angels, and will then repay every man according to his deeds. (Matthew 16:24-27)

When people heard these words of Jesus, and Him using slavery terminology, they knew exactly what He was calling for and that's why only a few out of the masses followed Him. What He was saying was that it required altogether a full commitment to Him, and in this, they had to deny self, giving up all rights and options, and follow a new Master. The ideas that have crept into the church concerning self-esteem, self worth, etc, all go directly against the biblical view of a Christian. It is just another ploy of Satan to deflect the believer away from the truth. Slaves are bought by their Master and it is now their desire to do the Master's will. Anyone denying this could easily fall into the hands of the master of darkness, Satan, being ever so deceived. This is the gospel, to deny yourself, take up the cross—that is, die to yourself—and follow Him as your new Master. This terminology of believers being slaves is used over 130 times in the New Testament.

Jesus said many times to other listeners, "Count the cost." Every person must realize it's not going to be easy to follow Him, that it will cost you your life, and you will be a slave to a new Master. And what Jesus asks us to do actually goes against everything our society tells us concerning self-will, self-improvement, self-determination and striving to be number one.

If anyone wishes to come after Me, he must deny himself, and take up his cross and follow Me. (Matthew 16:24)

Every person in every generation chooses. And in this choosing there are usually three groups of people. The first group is those who, right up front, deny Christ and take a hard stance against Him. The second group, which is the largest, is made up of those who say they believe in God, read His Word once in a while, but in God's view are just as lost as those who reject Him outright. They are not slaves of Christ but onlookers from a distance. *"But wait,"* you may ask, *"I believe in God and read the Bible."* Just because you believe in God and read the Bible doesn't make you a slave! Everyone in hell right now believes in God and knows without any doubt that God's Word is true. They also have a relationship with God—it's just not a good one. A true slave submits to the will of the Master and obeys Him with no options.

You believe that God is one. You do well; the demons also believe, and shudder. (James 2:19)

So, in looking at this biblical picture, the person who is a prodigal living in outright sin is not a Christian.

They went out from us, but they were not really of us; for if they had been of us, they would have remained with us; but they went out, so that it would be shown that they all are not of us. (1 John 2:19)

They are labeled sinners. This term is used biblically for the lost. They habitually walk in sin, not in righteousness. True believers, even though they still sin, habitually strive with the help of the Spirit for a righteous life. The sinner, being lost, is acting upon all he has—the flesh. Therefore he or she speaks and acts as a lost person. Thus the term prodigal may be used. So, in biblical terms, a prodigal is a not Christian. He may be religious now, or he may even have once been religious, but shows no fruit of true repentance or regeneration. In a very real sense, a true Christian should be obviously just that—a Christian. Christians love and serve the Lord from a heart of love, compassion, and a desire to please Him above all else; they are true slaves to the Master.

But what of the believer who wanders away for a season into a sinful lifestyle? How are we to treat such a person? This kind of situation is the most difficult. It's one thing for a person to deny Christ, walk away from the faith and declare openly an allegiance to the world and ultimately to Satan. It's altogether more confusing for a person to live in this season of sin and still claim to be a Christian; that's difficult to deal with! So, what do we do? There are several things.

First and foremost, pray, not only for yourself but also for that person. Unfortunately for his feelings, what will probably bring him back is affliction. God will use this to break him. If times are good and the lifestyle is being supported with plenty of money, repentance doesn't seem that feasible. So God may orchestrate things in such a way that bad times will come along until there is nothing left but to look up. Sadly it takes this to turn a person around to true repentance. This is also where the church may be of help. Where the situation involves a local body of believers who practice accountability among its members and church discipline, this will make a tremendous impact, not only on the person walking in sin but also in support for you, the member, through prayer, counsel, guidance, fellowship, love and the outworking of a team effort. In cases like this, sometimes the situation could be a long season, so having the leaders in the church come alongside to help becomes a great family affair of support. Biblically, though, there does appear to be a progression that can occur for the believer who takes the path of a sinful lifestyle. Let's take a look at this in detail and seek to understand this path of affliction.

- They usually have been warned: *"The way of the treacherous is hard"* (Proverbs 13:15). When you talk to them, warn them. So many times people become embarrassed, shy or fearful and don't speak the truth in love towards them. They need to be told the truth in the hope that this will bring about repentance.
- As believers, they are grieving the Spirit: *"Do not grieve the Holy Spirit of God, by whom you were sealed for the day of redemption."* (Ephesians 4:30). The Spirit indwells them and thus when they choose to sin, God the Spirit has the divine, emotional response of grieving. Why? Because He sees everything being done and He knows the consequences of it all. The believer walking in habitual sin daily grieves the indwelling Spirit; thus the Spirit will do a work to bring about repentance that will be perfectly fitted for that person in affliction.
- They go on sinning anyway: *"Therefore, to one who knows the right thing to do and does not do it, to him it is sin."* (James 4:17). Even though they've been warned and continue to grieve the Spirit, sometimes they continue to walk in habitual sin. It is at this point things may turn sour, not only in the conscience but in the details of their daily lives. Things usually start falling apart, perhaps financially, relationally, emotionally or physically.
- Bring in church discipline. (Matthew 18). This is where it is so sad when this vital part is left out, either because the

family or friends keep the situation away from the church's knowledge or the church itself doesn't practice this. The person walking in sin must know that he or she will be held accountable by other believers. Such people may associate with those who are also walking in sin and give heartfelt approval for their behavior, but as far as believers are concerned, they should be facing them and challenging them with their sinful lifestyle!

- As time moves on, they will eventually fall into being a slave to certain sins in their lives (Romans 6:20-23). This in itself will be a part of God's discipline. He will use this as a tool as a backlash to the believer. As an example of this, consider a friend of mine who made money his idol. God used this to discipline him in such a way that he lost everything and this eventually brought him back to God in repentance.

- What happens to someone who knows the ways of the Lord, yet turns away over and over toward a sinful lifestyle? If people continue to harden their hearts toward repentance, they can be delivered over to Satan for the destruction of their flesh (1 Corinthians 5:5, 11:30, 1 John 5:16-17) so as to prevent them from further hurt to themselves and others around them. This is decided by God Himself.

FINDING THE REAL YOU
THE FAITH TEST

Maria was a person who said she was a Christian, and really meant it. In fact, when she was asked about this, she would become angry and curse! But did she have a real biblical faith? Of course not! People from all over the world, in all kinds of faiths, claim to have some kind of faith in God, guiding and empowering them to do certain things in this life. The issue for the reader is "Am I truly a Christian?" As we have seen from our previous study, if you're not a slave to Christ, and born again (John 3:3-5), you're simply not truly saved. Maybe you are just very religious in times of trouble. But religion will not get you to heaven. Hell is full of religious people—only now it's too late for them. But for the troubled person, your judgment hasn't come yet. There is still time to repent and come to Christ.

The next section is for those who will honestly look at their heart and life, and compare it to how God describes a true believer. Sometimes what you think and what is true can be miles apart. Basically, two obvious things in your life will show whether or not you are a true Christian. The first will be the internal evidence of the Spirit's work of sanctification. The second will be the external evidence in one's behavior brought about by the internal change of regeneration by the indwelling Spirit—if you are born again, the Holy Spirit ensures that your life visibly shows the changes He is making in your life. Let's consider the internal evidence first. Take the test below and see how you do.

INTERNAL EVIDENCES TESTED

Take some time and read the Letter of 1 John. Then answer the following questions honestly, searching your heart for the truth about your relationship with the Lord. Answer with Y/N in the check-boxes.

☐ I have a deep desire to worship God.

☐ I love to commune with the Father daily in prayer.

☐ I look forward to reading God's Word and seeing how He wants me to think and live.

☐ I am very serious about my sin and seek to apply God's Word to it in order to change and practice His ways.

☐ I'm growing in my desire to be holy and pure in thought, motives and actions.

☐ I do not hate others, but am growing to love others as God loves me.

☐ I desire more than anything to be Christlike.

☐ I am willing to give up anything in following Christ.

☐ I am content.

☐ I am honest.

☐ I am forgiving.

☐ I see others as more important than myself.

Look up the following verses and write out what they teach:

Galatians 5:16

....

....

....

Ephesians 5:18

....

....

....

John 16:13

....

....

....

1 Thessalonians 5:19

....

....

....

Galatians 5:25

....

....

....

Ephesians 4:30

....

....

....

Hebrews 13:5

....

....

....

Romans 14:17-19

....

....

....

EXTERNAL EVIDENCES TESTED

Now that you've looked honestly at your heart and life, let's look at your lifestyle.

Consider the following questions and see if there is an outward demonstration that shows the effects of the work of God's Holy Spirit within you in bringing about the new birth.

And keep in mind this very important principle: These outward evidences should be an indication of the Holy Spirit's work within your heart, not just the things that show outwardly in your life. External religious behavior may make one appear saved, giving that person a false hope, when in reality all that has happened is that a few external are being kept.

1. I see a lessening of sinful behavior and more righteous behavior in my daily life:_____

2. The way I dress shows that I do not want to draw attention to myself but instead to have others see a difference in my life by godliness:____

3. My life is growing in practical discipline, cleanliness, and respectful observance of other people: ____

4. As the Holy Spirit works in my life, I see Him bringing order out of my chaotic lifestyle:_____ If not, what is it that is in the way?_____

5. Ask three people who know you well the following question: *"Do you see my lifestyle as one that is a good example of Christlikeness?"*

(Ask those three people to be honest and open toward you in their answer.)

First person's name...

Relationship ....

Answer ....

Why?...

Second person's name...

Relationship ....

Answer ....

Why?...

Third person's name..

Relationship ....

Answer ....

Why?...

Place a check-mark (or Y/N) in the squares below that apply to you:

☐   People see me as more loving and forgiving toward others.

☐   I do not smoke and drink.

☐   I do not flirt with the opposite sex if I'm married.

☐ I am honest in filing details in my tax returns.

☐ I work on my job as though Jesus were my boss.

☐ I treat everyone, no matter what race, color or religion they are, with respect and dignity.

☐   I do not use vulgarity or cursing language.

☐   No one can blame me for something sinful.

☐ I enjoy the fellowship of other believers.

☐ I do not steal from work or business.

☐ I do not gossip about others.

Look up the following verses and write out what they teach.

Titus 2:7

....

....

....

2 Thessalonians 3:7

....

....

....

1 Timothy 3:2

....

....

....

1 Thessalonians 2:10

....

....

....

1 Timothy 5:22

....

....

....

1 Thessalonians 3:7

....

....

....

Ephesians 4:2

....

....

....

Romans 12:17

....

....

....

1 Thessalonians 4:11-12

....

....

....

Matthew 5:44

....

....

....

1 Corinthians 9:25

....

....

....

Romans 14:1-23

....

....

....

Titus 2:14

....

....

....

Galatians 6:2

....

....

....

Acts 11:14, 30

....

....

....

Acts 2:42

....

....

....

1 Thessalonians 5:11

....

....

....

All of these internal desires and attributes will be in a truly born-again believer, and their *external behavior will be the fruit of their new birth.* If you are a troubled person and have been open and honest with yourself and with God, did you find out the truth about yourself? People who have been regenerated by the Holy Spirit exhibit a real change, and they have new desires and a new perspective on life. Instead of seeing the world as revolving around themselves—this is selfishness—they should now see things the way Christ sees them. They should be growing to be more *"others oriented."* All of these principles are found in the Gospel of John, Chapter 4, and the Letter of 1 John. The Spirit's goal is to bring about Christlikeness in the believer. Look up the following verses and write out what they teach about this issue of Christlikeness.

2 Corinthians 3:18

....

....

....

2 Corinthians 5:14-17

....

....

....

Galatians 5:22-23

....

....

....

Romans 8:1-17

....

....

....

Philippians 3:20-21

....

....

....

Lastly, look at the following verses and see how important this issue is concerning the Spirit and salvation. Are the things below really true of you?

For those who are according to the flesh set their minds on the things of the flesh, but those who are according to the Spirit, the things of the Spirit. (Romans 8:5)

For all who are being led by the Spirit of God, these are sons of God. (Romans 8:14)

Beloved, do not believe every spirit, but test the spirits to see whether they are from God...
(1 John 4:1)

You are from God, little children, and have overcome them;
because greater is He who is in you than he who is in the
world. (1 John 4:4).

By this the children of God and the children of the devil are
obvious: anyone who does not practice righteousness is not
of God, nor the one who does not love his brother.
(1 John 3:10)

These are the ones who cause divisions, worldly-minded,
devoid of the Spirit. (Jude 19)

It is clear that people who have the Spirit of God exhibit
certain fruit in their life that proves they are truly saved and
the Spirit dwells within them. After looking at all these Scriptures, does your life clearly reveal a person who walks in the
flesh or the Spirit? 1 John gives us a clear picture of how we
can truly know we are saved and indwelt by the Spirit.

The one who keeps His commandments abides in Him, and
He in him. We know by this that He abides in us, by the
Spirit whom He has given us. (1 John 3:24)

How can we know we are saved and that we have the Spirit?
There are several things in the verses listed above that can give
one the assurance of salvation.

THE GOSPEL IS REAL

When a person comes to Christ, part of this act of salvation
involves God the Father sending the Spirit to dwell within the
believer permanently. He regenerates, changing him with new
desires which allow him to overcome sin and practice right-

eousness. It's quite obvious he can't see the Holy Spirit—because He is a Spirit. Jesus said this in John 3 when He compared the Spirit to the wind. You can't see wind, but you can see its effects. So it is with the believer and the presence of the Spirit—one should see the effects or fruits in that person's life. In 1 John 4:14-15, the Apostle John says, *"We have seen and testify that the Father has sent the Son to be the Savior of the world. Whoever confesses that Jesus is the Son of God, God abides in him, and he in God."* How does a person know he or she has the Spirit? Not by some feeling, visions, or the hearing of voices. In biblical terms, they know they have the Spirit because they believe the facts—that the Father has sent the Son to be the Savior of the world, and they have confessed that He is their only Savior. They have humbled themselves, repented of their sinful past, and fully turned to Christ for salvation. The actual belief in the gospel is thus evidence of the presence of the Spirit in that person's life. People, on their own, could never accomplish this.

> *But a natural man[6] does not accept the things of the Spirit of God, for they are foolishness to him; and he cannot understand them, because they are spiritually appraised.*
> *(1 Corinthians 2:14)*

God's love shows itself in your life

A true believer comes to understand and to believe that God gave them His Spirit because of His eternal love for them, *"And we have known and believed the love that God has for us."* God is love; His nature is one of love. But the verse goes on, *"We have*

---

[6] Someone who is lost, a person who is not yet a Christian

105

come to know and have believed the love which God has for us. God is love, and the one who abides in love abides in God, and God abides in him." (1 John 4:16). You should understand three things about this love God has imparted to true believers.

- You have to understand and believe God the Father and who He is.
- You have to believe the Son and that He is God—that He is the Savior of the world, and that people need to be saved from their sin—and that He is Lord and Master.
- That by faith in Christ alone a sinner comes to God for salvation.

The final test, according to verse 16, is that you *"love"* God and it shows in your daily life. True believers don't love the world system, but their love is for God, for others, even for their enemies. This is the behavior/moral test. Every believer needs to look honestly into his own heart and see if these things are there. This is where the Marias of this world fail the test. The one way to discern real Christians is to note their outstanding love for others; it flows from their speech, thoughts and lives. They are not so concerned for themselves as they are for others. Not so with Maria. In talking with her, her needs, desires and wants were central. Some love was there if it somehow brought her something in return. But God's kind of love really wasn't present.

Fear of Judgment?

Love is also our confidence in judgment before God (1 John 4:17-18). When a person comes to Christ, the love of God is shed abroad in his heart. When that kind of perfected love is within, one can have confidence on the Day of Judgment. 1 John 2:28 reads, *"Now, little children, abide in Him, so that when*

He appears, we may have confidence and not shrink away from Him in shame at His coming." For the true believer, there is no fear at this event, but, instead, an expectation of great hope. Because of the evidence of love in our lives and obedience to His Word, we can go into the presence of God with boldness and confidence because all will be well!

The last statement in 1 John 4:17 is amazing. *"...because as He is, so also are we in this world."* The Father will treat us the same way He treats the Son. As Jesus is, in the eyes of the Father, so God sees us. Because we have been covered in Christ's righteousness, we can stand before God as our loving and caring Father. 1 John 3:2 reads, *"Beloved, now we are children of God, and it has not appeared as yet what we will be. We know that when He appears, we will be like Him, because we will see Him just as He is."*

While here on earth, we can't tell what we will be in perfection, but we will be like Him at His coming. For now we have been given God's love in our hearts, which superimposes itself over our old natures. In God's act of causing us to be born again, this new love grows and matures—is perfected—as we grow in our devotion to God and in obedience to His Word. If there is a lack of love for God and others, and fear in your life about when Christ returns, it just might mean you're not a real Christian at all. If you lack true love, forgiveness of others, or have little desire for holiness, this is a sign you are not truly saved.

WORSHIP

The Spirit helps us worship God (John 4:23-24). Only the born-again believer, one who has put his faith in Christ, can rightly worship God. Jesus made this very clear to the apostles and believers throughout history.

But an hour is coming, and now is, when the true worshipers will worship the Father in spirit and truth; for such people the Father seeks to be His worshipers. God is spirit, and those who worship Him must worship in spirit and truth. (John 4:23-24)

It must also be mentioned that many around the world worship "God" or some other form of a god. Yet God has made a righteous path to Himself through Christ the only Messiah. The road to hell is probably marked *"the religious way,"* yet it leads to destruction.

"This people honors Me with their lips,
But their heart is far away from Me.
"But in vain do they worship Me,
Teaching as doctrines the precepts of men."
(Matthew 15:8-9)

If you have no real desire to worship God, then you need to search your heart to see if you are a true believer. And ask yourself an all important heart-searching question. Practically, what do I really worship? In other words, where are most of my time and desires directed? Sports, money, hobbies, fame or other people? A Spirit-indwelt believer will want to worship Him. In the verse above, Jesus was quoting Isaiah 29:13. Through all of human history, man has been motivated to create his own way to God. It started in Genesis 11 with the tower of Babel and continued in the land of Israel among the delivered people of God. Jesus confronted man-directed worship again during His ministry on earth, and it is still prevalent today. For the troubled person who is lost, you will have little desire to worship God because of your alienation from Him.

PRAYER

The Spirit gives us the right and ability to pray. Many people in numerous different religions pray, but only those who are truly born again and have the Spirit dwelling within have the right and the ability to pray and have those prayers accepted and answered by God according to His divine will. Yet when there are lingering sins in your life, and your conscience continues to condemn you for it, you will find it very difficult to pray. But if you are a true believer and pray, the arena in which that occurs is tremendous. The Father in heaven is enthroned; our advocate Christ (who is our divine lawyer, Hebrews 4:14-16; 1 John 2:1), is sitting at the right hand of the Father, pleading our prayers before the Father; and the Spirit, who is our intercessor, likewise pleads our prayers before Christ. In this divine interaction, our prayers come before God, who answers them, either with the response, "Yes," or "No," or, sometimes, "Wait." He always gives us what is best for His purpose, His glory, and our ultimate good. This part is critical to true spiritual growth in one's life.

Only a true believer has a desire to pray and commune with God because of the close relationship. Maria, on the other hand, had a hard time praying because she didn't have a clear conscience and she had no personal relationship with Christ. Instead, her prayers were seen as ritualistic, as though she was praying to a God far off, a God not listening. In 1 Thessalonians 5:17, Paul the Apostle says, "Pray without ceasing." To *pray without ceasing* refers to recurring prayer, not nonstop talking. Prayer is to be a way of life. You're to be continually in an attitude of prayer. It is living in ongoing God-consciousness, lived in deep awareness of and surrender to Jesus as Lord. It should be an intimate communication.

To *"pray without ceasing"* means when you are troubled or tempted, you hold the temptation before God and ask for His help. When you experience something good and beautiful, you immediately thank the Lord for it. When you see evil around you, you ask God to make it right and to use you possibly to help end it. When you meet someone who does not know Christ, you pray for God to draw that person to Himself and to use you as a faithful instrument to be an effective witness. Thus life becomes a continually ascending prayer: all life's thoughts, deeds, and circumstances become an opportunity to commune with your Heavenly Father. In that way, you constantly set your mind *"on the things above, not on the things that are on earth"* (see Colossians 3:1-2). (You're one who walks in the flesh less and moves, talks and thinks in the Spirit, being obedient to the Word.)

With all prayer and petition pray at all times in the Spirit, and with this in view, be on the alert with all perseverance and petition for all the saints. (Ephesians 6:18)

In the same way the Spirit also helps our weakness; for we do not know how to pray as we should, but the Spirit Himself intercedes for us with groanings too deep for words; and He who searches the hearts knows what the mind of the Spirit is, because He intercedes for the saints according to the will of God. (Romans 8:26-27)

Keeping on keeping on

Therefore, my beloved brethren, be steadfast, immovable, always abounding in the work of the Lord, knowing that your toil is not in vain in the Lord. (1 Corinthians 15:58)

One of the evidences that you are truly saved is that you are still striving to be Christlike, even after a period of hard times and afflictions, whether these are internal and external. In contrast, a *"religious"* person goes on living a dual kind of lifestyle: one of continual, habitual sinning, with little change toward Christlikeness in his life, yet still believing in God (James 2:19) in an intellectual way. For such people, when hard times come along, their lives usually fall apart; chaos rules and sin abounds. They may even use sinful means to get out of those hard times by lying, deceiving or even hurting others. But for true believers, their ways of reacting to hard times will be through trust, perseverance in doing what is right. They can easily see the Spirit working and slowly guiding their lives and growth toward being Christlike in the responses to suffering. Sometimes there is an awe and amazement to see all the things God has done within them during the course of time. He has been faithful to continue the sanctification process when they were not all that faithful.

Now, take a few moments and look up the following verses and write out what each teaches.

Ephesians 6:18

....

....

....

John 10:28-29

....

....

....

Romans 11:29

....

....

....

Philippians 1:6

....

....

....

1 Peter 1:5

....

....

....

Job 17:9

....

....

....

John 15:9

....

....

....

Acts 13:43

....

....

....

Romans 2:7

....

....

....

Galatians 6:9

....

....

....

2 Timothy 3:16

....

....

....

Hebrews 12:1

....

....

....

1 Peter 1:13

....

....

....

Revelation 3:11

....

....

....

APPLICATION PROJECTS: WEEK #3

In this week's personal application project, you were asked to take the faith test in the book. In doing that, you were assigned to ask a few people some questions about you and your faith. You can continue to do that throughout the coming days as you move on to week four and five. You don't have to wait to complete this assignment before moving on.

1 If Jesus is Lord, what does that mean from our readings today?

....

....

....

2 If we are slaves of Christ, what does that mean from our readings today?

....

....

....

....

3 Stop and think through this. Make a list of things you know you have done that shows Christ wasn't your Master.

....

....

....

....

4 Last week you memorized Matthew 16:24-27. What have you learned from this verse about you and the Lord?

....

....

....

....

5 What things in your life prevent you from giving all up to follow Christ? What personal desires are a roadblock to truly following Christ? What is of more value than Christ?

....

....

....

....

6 What does it mean in Luke 14:28-33 when Jesus says *"Count the cost"*?

....

....

....

7 Read James 2:19. What is James teaching us here in this context?

....

....

....

8 After taking the faith test in the book, explain what you have learned about yourself.

....

....

....

9 Memorize Luke 10:27.

4

How Can I Change So That It Lasts?

WEEK FOUR

Maria loved her sin even though she denied it and said she was a Christian. But how you live, spend your money or time, and treat others—including your enemies—shows what you really love and whom you follow. Maria, in reality, loved her sin and refused to die to her own selfish desires and live fully for Christ. This is the great divide between a true believer and a pretend believer. For true believers, biblically driven change should be a part of their daily lives until they breathe their last. It is never viewed as just for the young. Change should always be one's personal goal, even through hard times.

> *I spoke to you in your prosperity;*
> *But you said, "I will not listen!"*
> *This has been your practice from your youth,*
> *That you have not obeyed My voice. (Jeremiah 22:21)*

Over the years, I've found two basic reasons why people don't change. First, they are unwilling because their sin is either more important to them in practice than God is, and they are acting in rebellion, or they may not know how to change. They feel stuck in a trap with no way out. They should realize they can't change the past, but they can change their present situation. If they choose to dwell on the past and live presently with all that bitterness, change will never occur. The past is gone and can't be changed; rather, they themselves need to change! The past can only be dealt with in the present by the exercise of forgiveness, reconciliation, and repentance. Repentance, a changing of direction, is a change of mind and motives that leads to a change in lifestyle (see Acts 20:26). One's aim as a Christian is to please and glorify God, to press on daily with the following goal in mind:

Brethren, I do not regard myself as having laid hold of it yet; but one thing I do: forgetting what lies behind and reaching forward to what lies ahead, I press on toward the goal for the prize of the upward call of God in Christ Jesus. (Philippians 3:13-14).

But you want changes that last? It is the goal of this book to direct you toward change, but ultimately that change must come from your heart and from the Spirit's work in your life. Let me explain how it all works in practice: People develop habits of sinful thinking and behavior that lead to so much trouble in their lives. They must have a desire for dehabituation and rehabituation, or to put it a simpler way, need to develop a "Put-off/Put-on" mindset as found in Ephesians 4. Things they used to do habitually they are to put off—or cease doing—and put on new ways of living instead.

Your manner of life is a habitual way of life. God gave us all a gift called habit. But, because sin came into this world (see Genesis 3), we all can easily and naturally choose sinful ways that, over time, can develop into bad, life patterns of habitual sins.

For everyone who partakes only of milk is not accustomed to the word of righteousness, for he is an infant. But solid food is for the mature, who because of practice have their senses trained to discern good and evil. (Hebrews 5:13-14)

We all need to be taught that if we practice what God tells us, and live obediently to His principles, the habit will become a part of our lives. In actuality, choosing to follow God's principles brings discipline into our lives, along with blessings and eternal life.

The diagram below illustrates how habits are put off and put on for Christians, all through the power of the Spirit in obedience to the Word of God. Sinful habits are put off daily by intently saying no to them, no matter how you feel, and instead intently putting on and applying the biblical way in every situation. This applies to the areas of relationships, money, morality and every other area of your life.

HABITUATION

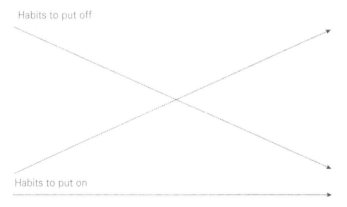

Habits to put off

Habits to put on

Habituation: Learning habits, by practice—good or bad

Putting it into practice

YOUR PERSONAL HABITUATION LISTS

Take a few moments and fill in the blanks below. Write out what things in your life you should put off, then on the opposite side write out the things you are to put on and practice daily.

122

Put-off List ....**Put-on List**

....

....

....

....

Therefore, laying aside falsehood, speak truth each one of you with his neighbor, for we are members of one another. Be angry, and yet do not sin; do not let the sun go down on your anger, and do not give the devil an opportunity. He who steals must steal no longer; but rather he must labor, performing with his own hands what is good, so that he will have something to share with one who has need. Let no unwholesome word proceed from your mouth, but only such a word as is good for edification according to the need of the moment, so that it will give grace to those who hear. Do not grieve the Holy Spirit of God, by whom you were sealed for the day of redemption. Let all bitterness and wrath and anger and clamor and slander be put away from you, along with all malice. Be kind to one another, tender-hearted, forgiving each other, just as God in Christ also has forgiven you. (Ephesians 4:25-32)

But now you also, put them all aside: anger, wrath, malice, slander, and abusive speech from your mouth. Do not lie to one another, since you laid aside the old self with its evil practices, and have put on the new self who is being re-

newed to a true knowledge according to the image of the One who created him—a renewal in which there is no distinction between Greek and Jew, circumcised and uncircumcised, barbarian, Scythian, slave and freeman, but Christ is all, and in all. So, as those who have been chosen of God, holy and beloved, put on a heart of compassion, kindness, humility, gentleness and patience; bearing with one another, and forgiving each other, whoever has a complaint against anyone; just as the Lord forgave you, so also should you. Beyond all these things put on love, which is the perfect bond of unity. (Colossians 3:8-14)

In the verses above, we see the put-off/put-on principle of Scripture. As fallen creatures saved by the pure grace of God, we are to put off the old ways and put on and practice the Christlike ways in every area of life. Through the power of the Spirit and obedience to the Word of God, you are commanded to *change* for the glory of God. For Maria, she changed too, but for the worse. This kind of lifestyle takes little effort. For the sinful religious person, things never ultimately get better, but the inner conflicts of a guilty conscience and outward circumstances get more difficult as the years pass. For people like Maria, not only is she a bad testimony to others by calling herself a Christian, but her definition of a believer creates a lack of hope, direction and despair for anyone thinking like her.

THE FEELING-ORIENTED PERSON

Allowing feelings to rule your decision-making process is a huge problem among people. I don't think there has been one counseling situation over the years where this was not a part of the problem. Almost every person I have ever counseled has been living a feeling-orientated kind of lifestyle. Their biblically uninformed decisions, based on their feelings, cause harmful repercussions for many people they know. God gave us feelings and emotions for a very good reason. The problem comes when we let them run our lives, making foolish decisions based upon the feelings of the moment. A person who is feeling-oriented will live a life much like a roller coaster; ups and downs will become a lifestyle. Eventually people like this become very emotionally disturbed and are usually labeled, at the extremes, *bi-polar* by the medical and psychological professions. In reality, for the prodigal, a bi-polar person is no more than one who has been trained to live by his or her emotions, making decisions and letting their twisted minds be shoved back and forth according to how they feel. There is no discernment, no wise principles used in the making of decisions based upon God's Word, but rather a situation of just floating along making one wrong decision after another, causing more and more harm to themselves and to others. Slowly they build thought patterns that create wrong decisions, like building blocks of destruction.

> *But if any of you lacks wisdom, let him ask of God, who gives to all generously and without reproach, and it will be given to him. But he must ask in faith without any doubting, for the one who doubts is like the surf of the sea, driven and tossed by the wind. For that man ought not to expect that he will receive anything from the Lord, being a double-minded man, unstable in all his ways. (James 1:5-8)*

This kind of feeling-oriented prodigal is one of the main reasons so many have outbursts of anger, are greedy, and experience much by way of bitterness and lust problems. They have trained themselves incorrectly in their thinking. By the time they come for counseling, they feel trapped, as if there is no hope. The key to true biblical change in a person's life is to realize the harm of the feeling-oriented lifestyle. Such a person needs to become a person who is commandment-oriented, being steadfastly obedient to God's Word no matter how he feels; that is critical for spiritual growth.

You might be saying to yourself, *"Not me, I could never do that"*. But God says you can! In fact, He commands you to be that way:

No temptation has overtaken you but such as is common to man; and God is faithful, who will not allow you to be tempted beyond what you are able, but with the temptation will provide the way of escape also, so that you will be able to endure it. (1 Corinthians 10:13)

"... the Lord knows how to rescue the godly from temptation, and to keep the unrighteous under punishment for the day of judgment." (2 Peter 2:9)

God will never tell a believer to do something that cannot be done. The problem is not with God; it's with you and your own desires.

The feeling-oriented person:
Getting it backwards

The kite illustration represents our lives and the decision-making processes, all of which can cause us to fall into many destructive, sinful traps if we fail to live according to biblical principles. This is how most prodigals become such; this is a common attribute of their thinking. The man in the diagram represents the thinking process. The kite itself represents behavior, which is greatly affected by the man's thinking. He may turn the kite any way he wishes. The tail of the kite, which moves according to where the kite itself goes, represents our feelings. The kite illustration reveals how things are supposed to operate when we make decisions. A situation comes our way in which we need to make a decision; it could be relational, financial or it could be a moral issue. We do what is right according to God's Word and principles, no matter how we feel. This thought pattern affects how we act, and in turn affects our feelings to make them align with our actions. If anyone trains himself to respond to life this way, there will be much blessing. This may include spiritual maturity, wise living, the absence of afflictions arising from wrong choices, and you will be seen by others as steadfast, one who can be trusted. But what most people do is the opposite. They make decisions based upon how they feel, in the moment, which leads to broken relationships, financial hardships and to becoming a person who is impulsive, sins habitually, and is just the opposite of how God directs people to live. Below are some principles to live by in this area.

- *Become aware of sinful practices that must be put off in your life.* You must look into your own life and honestly see what sinful things you are doing and what good things you are not doing, and discover how Christ wants you to change.
- *Find the biblical alternative.* You must find out from Scripture what Christ wants you to replace for the things you put off. Let me give an example. Suppose a person has a lying problem. What is needed is for that person to replace it with truth telling.
- *Restructure your life for change.* What places, events or situations in your life need to change to help you have a clear conscience, good testimony and Christlike responses?
- *Break away from impediments that have the effect of making sin easier.* What influences do you have in your life that tempt you to sin?
- *Be accountable to others for change—no lone rangers.* Find someone in your church you can have as a discipler who will hold you accountable for change. A person who wants to hide his or her sin will not want to be accountable. A de-

sire to be a lone ranger is a sign that a person really doesn't want to change much (Proverbs 18:1).

- *Stress spiritual growth.* This should be your ultimate goal every day.
- *Daily practice biblical habits, being responsible, being consistent.*
- *From a pure heart, seek to glorify God in all you do, say or think.* Realize though that temptation will always come from within your heart and from without by the world. The key is in choosing to practice the right biblical choices in your life.

APPLICATION PROJECTS: WEEK #4

1 According to this week's reading, why is it hard for people to change?

....

....

....

2 Once you have filled out your "Put-off/Put-on" list, explain how you are going to put into practice those good things.

....

....

....

3 Read James 1:14-15. What things in your life lure you away into sin? What does the Bible say about those sins?

....

....

....

4 Have you been diagnosed with a syndrome, illness or disease? If so, what is the label?

....

....

....

(Buy and read *Blame it on the Brain* by Dr. Edward Welch.[7])

5 What is the one area in your life that will be the hardest to change? Take some time and search the Scriptures as to what God says about this area.

....

....

....

6 Memorize 2 Timothy 3:16-17.

---

[7] Published by P&R Publishing Company, 1998

5

What Does the Lord Your God Require of You?

WEEK FIVE

"Now, Israel, what does the LORD your God require from you, but to fear the LORD your God, to walk in all His ways and love Him, and to serve the LORD your God with all your heart and with all your soul, and to keep the LORD's commandments and His statutes which I am commanding you today for your good?"
(Deuteronomy 10:12-13)

It is a stunning phenomenon to experience the presence of God coming upon any scene; the Bible records how people fainted, fell to their knees, trembled, grew scared, worshiped Him with great respect, and even fainted. These are just a few of the expressions used to picture the awesome presence, power, and personality of God. Mountains shook, clouds thundered, the earth split open, and people ran for shelter at His speaking to humans. God, the creator of everything that exists—the originator of everything from the tiniest atom to the largest star in the skies—took interest in the creation of mankind. Yet, it is man who always seems to fear Him the least. The One who gives every breath, who has decided how many days each one shall live and knows everything about us, is the very One most ignored, least respected, least obeyed and, most of all, least feared.

The verses quoted above speak about the blessings of obeying God. Here God makes it clear what is expected of us all. And if we can't answer this question about what God expects, we are in a perilous place, with eternal consequences! And in all this, the question must be asked, *"What does God require?"* It's not a suggestion, and neither is it an option. This is what He requires. And one of the dangerous aspects of life for any prodigal is this lack of fear of God. Little do prodigals realize the stark reality that He is watching, planning and acting to either bring about a sincere repentance using afflictions custom fit for them or bringing judgment. It is much like the fool who was on a large boat, drinking, laughing and dancing on the deck while both sides of the ship were burning, the flames slowly creeping towards him, sinking the boat in the frigid arctic waters. People on an adjacent lifeboat were yelling at him to leave and come with those being saved from the soon-coming doom, but, no, he just laughed, snickering at their warnings. Not too soon later, he found himself alone, in the frigid waters, drowning, overcome by hypothermia. So it is with prodigals, or any other people for that matter, who lack a healthy fear of God. They are the fools also. A lack of this fear brings about foolish decisions and total blindness to God's discipline in their lives. So let's look at the five things God requires.

1. Fear the Lord Your God. It's good that these requirements start with the heart attitude; it's only right because it's from here that motives are brought out to affect one's lifestyle.

The fear of the LORD is the beginning of wisdom,
And the knowledge of the Holy One is understanding.
(Proverbs 9:10)

Worship the LORD with reverence
And rejoice with trembling. (Psalm 2:11)

This fear of God is an awestruck feeling of deep reverence, at who He is and His power. It is coming into His presence, realizing you could be totally vaporized in a blink of an eye. The meaning of the Hebrew word for *"fear"* includes all these things but it also includes holy terror.

It is the LORD of hosts whom you should regard as holy.
And He shall be your fear,
And He shall be your dread. (Isaiah 8:13)

We truly live today in a world of fear, with all its *phobias*. Doctors and counselors work full time in trying to help people deal with their fears. Maybe you as a prodigal have certain fears. But do you fear God? You should! One of the greatest faults modern Christians have today is their lack of understanding about what it means to fear God. They live their Christian lives on the edges, living as though God is just a God of love and that He would not discipline them for sins because they are His children. He is more an appendage to their lives than Lord and Master. They fail to understand that God is a righteous judge and Father and will by no means let His own people go on sinning but will bring about an affliction, custom-fitted to bring about a sincere repentance. The real truth is this: the person who fears God will fear nothing else. But for the prodigal, a healthy fear of God is needed—yet the threat level is both high and real. It is a tragedy when someone who call himself a *Christian* lives, talks and acts in ways that are truly wrong and self-centered, yet thinks little of trouble due to sin. Such a person is saying, in effect, that God will not act.

Behold then the kindness and severity of God; to those who
fell, severity, but to you, God's kindness, if you continue in
His kindness; otherwise you also will be cut off.
(Romans 11:22)

Both God's graciousness and judgment work in perfect harmony; there is no injustice, unfairness or partiality. God is both a righteous judge and a redeemer for those who receive His free gift of salvation.

> *Therefore, having these promises, beloved, let us cleanse ourselves from all defilement of flesh and spirit, perfecting holiness in the fear of God. (2 Corinthians 7:1)*

We really can't fully know His love until we grasp the fear of the Lord as a balance in our lives. One without the other creates an imbalance that will either lead to a lifestyle uninhibited with sin, trusting that His grace will allow one to go on sinning, or a fear that allows for no grace. It is because prodigals act as they do that they are shallow in their understanding of this dynamic of fear. One who does not fear God is a fool.

2. We are to walk in all His ways. If a person has a healthy heart-felt attitude of a fear of God, will they desire to walk in His ways? They will study His Word, learning what His principles are so they may walk in them. This Hebrew word for *"walk"* speaks of our daily conduct, how we order our day, our words and deeds—these are all part of our walk. In them we seek to please God as we walk as Jesus walked. It is for His glory.

> *Therefore I, the prisoner of the Lord, implore you to walk in a manner worthy of the calling with which you have been called, with all humility and gentleness, with patience, showing tolerance for one another in love, being diligent to preserve the unity of the Spirit in the bond of peace. (Ephesians 4:1-3)*

Not only are we instructed to walk in God's ways, but we are told to teach the same to those around us. We are to be a godly influence, not a sinful one. As prodigals, your bad example is

137

screaming out to others as a picture of disgrace, a lack of fear of God with an uncaring, foolish attitude. Many other prodigals will gather around you to all act just as foolishly. (See Deuteronomy 6:2). It is truly the wise in heart who seek to follow His ways instead. For in them will come true guidance, peace and a sturdy foundation for life.

3. We are to love Him. This phraseology is used hundreds of times in the Bible and it is placed here in this verse right at the heart because it takes a heart of love for all He has done to rightly be obedient and to desire to walk in all His ways. The Hebrew word *"love"* is usually reserved for marital love. It is a word that speaks of deep sincerity, intimacy and closeness. It speaks of affection. It is not *"Do these things"* only; it is primarily for a person to love the Lord God and out of this will flow a desire to obey. Without a sincere love, all you have is a legalist. This is God's main concern—love! We are to love Him with all our heart and mind. Jesus said clearly that this was the greatest commandment.

> *You shall love the Lord your God with all your heart, with all your soul, and with all your strength. (See Deuteronomy 6:4, 7:9, 11:1, 13:3, Matthew 22:37, Luke 10:27.)*

This kind of love surpasses any other kind of love this world has to offer. This is the same kind of love that God has when He planned to save those who would believe on Him when He sent His own beloved Son to earth in order to suffer and die for the sins of those who would believe. That took a deep love. He not only demands our allegiance and loyalty, but He also demands our devotion and love. True Christianity is not a matter of externals, doing this, performing that. Rather, it all stems and flows from a heart of love for Him. And the key to life-discernment is a heart of love for God.

> *Moreover the LORD your God will circumcise your heart and the heart of your descendants, to love the LORD your God with all your heart and with all your soul, so that you may live. (Deuteronomy 30:6)*

4. We are to serve the Lord our God. This service flows from a heart of love that comes from your heart and soul. That makes service a joy. As a prodigal, you presently serve the desires of your sinful flesh, all stemming from selfishness. This comes from what you can get out of it rather than the opposite, all of which is what we've been talking about. A heart of love for Him will automatically give you a desire to serve others. God never wants us to serve Him in a robotic or legalistic way.

5. Keep the commandments of the Lord and His statutes...for your good. As a prodigal, you've often made decisions based upon what you thought was good for you. But those decisions in reality were both harmful and destructive to your life. Sin never blesses! All of the sayings of God are an example of God's grace, words to tell all prodigals to listen and obey so that they may truly live and avoid afflictions arising from sin. David the king of Israel was a man who went through much hardship in his life because of bad choices he had made. But consider what he says about God's Word and his obedience.

> *How can a young man keep his way pure?*
> *By keeping it according to Your word. (Psalm 119:9)*

> *Make me walk in the path of Your commandments,*

For I delight in it. (Psalm 119:35)

Before I was afflicted I went astray,
But now I keep Your word. (Psalm 119:67)

I would highly recommend the reading of Psalm 119 for the prodigal, for in it David expresses how important obeying God's Word was for real life. But understand the last phrase of this verse: *"Stiffen your neck no longer" (Deuteronomy 10:16b).* In all these five things God commanded us to do and live. We have a complete inability to carry those things out unless God enables us to do them—so how does He do that? By saving us through Christ our Savior! But you must come to Him repentant, seeking to follow Him the rest of your life. That's why He says in verse 15 *"Yet on your fathers did the LORD set His affection to love them, and He chose their descendants after them, even you above all peoples, as it is this day..."* But then He says stop being *stiff-necked* about it. This phrase is interesting. It could be used of the people in hell. They are stiff-necked. It speaks of stubbornness, an unwillingness to obey God but a foolish stubbornness to disobey and live as they want, leading to destruction. God says there needs to be an internal change of heart and that's only by God's grace through repentance. Oh prodigal, come to Him today.

THE POINT OF NO RETURN

Therefore God gave them over in the lusts of their hearts to impurity, so that their bodies would be dishonored among them. (Romans 1:24)

Throughout the many years I've been counseling, I've run across a phenomenon that has saddened my heart on many occasions. It is this reality: I've met many people who actually appeared to have no hope of change. They have let sin reign in their lives so long that it has actually warped their thinking to the point where it seems there is no return. The Bible is clear that God exists, that He has spoken, and that He holds every human accountable to what he has said and done. When people live most of their lives walking in habitual sin, even knowing the right way, there comes a point of no return—not because God isn't capable, but because people are stubbornly hardened to love this world and their sin more than anything else.

This was the path Maria chose. She was exposed to the gospel many times, had read her Bible, had gone to church on several occasions, and really believed there was a God, yet she continued to live a life of rebellion, deceit, greed, immorality, and held a twisted view of God and the accountability she owed Him with respect to her life. As I talked to her, it was clear that she viewed God as a very loving God, One who isn't judgmental. But the fact is that God does Judge sin, and the Bible is very clear about that. Even with true believers, He doesn't let them get away with habitual sin but will bring discipline into their lives to bring about a repentance and turning from sin. This is because He is a loving Father who really cares about our lives.

As time moved on, Maria's life became worse. More trouble followed her. Eventually she came to the point where she was totally engulfed in all the sinful practices of life. God has warned people throughout Scripture about sin's destructive ways. No one who claims to be a believer will ever be blessed while living in habitual sin. Do you want the blessing of God in your life? If you do, you must come to Christ as both Lord and Savior.

God gives us warnings about sin and its destructive ways in our lives. Maria was one who was facing this in her life through torn relationships, financial hardships, and emotional struggles within herself. Her life was hard, and trouble followed her daily. She would cry, weep, and get angry at God for all the trouble in her life, yet she failed to realize that what she was facing were the repercussions of her sin. Bad relationships, continual financial hardships, deceit from friends, and confusion and disorder followed her. This is the way it usually is for people who choose to walk in habitual sin.

But the way of the treacherous is hard. (Proverbs 13:15b)

Adversity pursues sinners. (Proverbs 13:21)

Maria, like so many others, knows right from wrong. God has placed this within every person. It's called a conscience, and everybody has one. It is something that God gives to people to help them know what is right and wrong, and how to live. The problem comes when people ignore this God-given conscience and choose to do what is wrong—things like deceit, theft, greed, immorality and all the other various kinds of sin. Continually choosing to follow sin's deceitful ways starts the process of searing one's conscience, making it hardened to right and wrong, leading to a place from where there may be no return.

Therefore, to one who knows the right thing to do and does not do it, to him it is sin. (James 4:17)

The Bible teaches that every human ever born is by nature a slave to sin. People have little desire to do righteousness on their own or to even please God. Even those who say they believe in God walk in habitual sin and are slaves to it. To be a slave means our desires and thoughts are geared toward pleasing the one enslaving us. Sin becomes the master of our lives and, even though we want to do well, we continue to choose evil and thus face the consequences.

... you are slaves of the one whom you obey...
(Romans 6:16)

Maria, even though she said she believed in God, showed by the fruit of her life that sin was her real master, and Satan was her real spiritual father. This is the common thread with most people in this kind of situation. They think by their mere belief in God all will be fine in the end. But the truth is they are still a slave to whom they obey. If they continue to walk in sin, then they are a slave. This is what the Apostle John was saying, *"Let no one deceive you. He who habitually practices righteousness is righteous just as He is righteous. He who habitually sins is of the devil for the devil has sinned from the beginning. Whoever has been born of God does not continually sin"* (See 1 John 3:7-8). This verse is important to understand. The lost remain under the wrath of God. What John is teaching here is one's pattern of life. For believers, before conversion, they were living only in the flesh and being guided by the flesh. Sin was as natural as breathing. They habitually sinned, walked and thought sinfully. But upon conversion, all that changed. The nature is regenerated, renewed by the presence of the Holy Spirit upon sincere repentance and turning to Christ. They are no longer a slave to sin. They have died to selfish desires and been spiritually resurrected to serve Christ and to do His will. That's the difference between true believers and people like Maria. True believers pursue holiness and righteousness in their lives, striving to be Christlike out of a love for what God has done for them. They no longer are to be known as those who habitually walk in sin, but in righteousness.

But those who say they are believers yet walk in habitual sins will face all kinds of hardships. That's what John is teaching here. What is the fruit of your life like? Are you pursuing holiness and purity in everything you do and say, or are you full of sin every day? Basically you have two choices. You can continue to play games and not get serious about your relationship with God, living in your sin, all of which leads toward a life full of destruction with little no hope. Or you can realize you are a sinner before a Holy God yet one who has a Redeemer. But the prerequisite is your willingness to give up your life and follow Him, having a desire to be Christlike in everything. If you choose this path, you will be blessed, have God's peace in your heart, and have His promise of living forever with him in total bliss. You choose.

IN CLOSING. . . WHO IS YOUR FATHER?

Have you ever thought about who your spiritual father is? Is it God the Father or is it Satan? You may be tempted to laugh, but this is a very serious question. If you're like Maria, believing in God yet lost, your father is Satan! This is an amazing reality. You might not have thought about it like this, but everyone in hell is religious today. They all know there is a God, they believe that this God exists, and to a certain point actually have more knowledge that God's Word is true than we do. Why? They are seeing the results—and that will last forever. Just believing that there is a God but not living a life of obedience to His Word are two different things.

144

If God is really your Father, you will see in your life a desire to live a pure, holy life, striving to please Him in everything you do. But if you're a slave to sin, the fruit of that in your life will be destruction, confusion and affliction. This is the great divide between the lost and the saved. This is why Jesus said the road leading to hell is wide and many are those who walk on that path but narrow is the road that leads to eternity with God and few are those who find it (Matthew 7:13). Which road are you going to walk on? What I am saying is as real as the words on this page; one day you will stand before God and give an account of your life. That is a sobering reality for anyone. Paul knew this very well, and he wrote about this in 1 Corinthians 11:31, *"But if we judged ourselves rightly, we would not be judged."* What an amazing statement and something I've been trying to teach the readers throughout this book. If you're honest with yourself and you judge yourself correctly, you will not face the judgment of God. Instead you will have peace in your heart and hope for the future if you're truly a believer. In this same chapter, of 1 Corinthians 11:30, Paul writes *"For this reason many among you are weak and sick, and a number sleep.[8]"* What Paul is teaching us here is that sin can be very destructive in a person's life, especially to those who say they're believers but continue to walk in habitual sin. They will be weak, sickly, and even die. That's why in verse 31 he directs us to judge ourselves correctly. Why? To avoid these things. But if you're like Maria who knew all about this but continued to live a life in sin, you will have to face the consequences of those choices.

---

[8] Sleep—a reference to having died.

APPLICATION PROJECTS: WEEK #5

1 Now that you have completed reading this book, answer in your own words, this question: What is a true Christian?

....

....

....

2 Can you say now that you have come to Christ on His terms and are willing to follow Him the rest of your life?

....

....

....

3 Read through the book of 1 John (not the Gospel of John) and write out a personal list of what a true Christian should be like.

....

....

....

4 If you have come to a true knowledge of Jesus Christ and have made the decision to follow Him, find a Bible-believing church and get involved.

....

....

....

5 Memorize 1 Chronicles 16:8-12.

Postscript

Answering the Most Important Question in Your Life

YOUR PERSONAL QUEST…

N ow that you've read this book—and hopefully have been very honest about who you are and what you are—you can now make a good evaluation of what you should know and what you need to do. What you do with this information will make all the difference in this life and the next. I pray that you, the reader, will not take this lightly or see your life as not being held accountable before God, because it will. These decisions, and the questions that surround them, are the most important ones you will ever face in your entire lifetime.

What are you going to do with Jesus Christ and His Word? It goes far beyond just believing in God; rather, it must go to the very core of your being! As has already been proven, your life is falling apart and trouble follows you, surrounding you like a morning fog—that's very obvious. Sin always leads to destruction, never to ultimate blessing. What I'm talking about is a daily, personal relationship with Jesus Christ and obedience to His Word, through the power of the Holy Spirit who indwells true believers. For most of your life, you've been walking in the flesh and the fruit of that is obvious: affliction and hard times have followed. If you still want to play games with your life and your relationship to Christ, then there is nothing more I could ever write. Maybe you haven't sunk deep enough in your troubles to look up to God. But, I can promise this, that if you choose to follow Jesus with a whole heart, there will be blessing, peace, contentment and direction in this life and the next. So, what will you do now?

Oh give thanks to the LORD, call upon His name;
Make known His deeds among the peoples.
Sing to Him, sing praises to Him;

Speak of all His wonders.
Glory in His holy name;
Let the heart of those who seek the LORD be glad.
Seek the LORD and His strength;
Seek His face continually.
Remember His wonderful deeds which He has done,
His marvels and the judgments from His mouth...
(1 Chronicles 16:8-12)